A JOHN CATT PUBLICATION

SUSTAINING RESILIENCE FOR
LEADERSHIP

Stories from education

How's the re-boot going?

Not good.
Think I need an upgrade.

JULIA STEWARD

Illustrations by Karen McMillan

First published 2018

by John Catt Educational Ltd,
12 Deben Mill Business Centre, Old Maltings Approach,
Melton, Woodbridge IP12 1BL

Tel: +44 (0) 1394 389850 Fax: +44 (0) 1394 386893
Email: enquiries@johncatt.com
Website: www.johncatt.com

ISBN: 978 1 911 382 84 3

Set and designed by John Catt Educational Limited

Praise for Sustaining Resilience

'Julia has written a wonderful and informative book on one of the most important aspects of performance in any field. Understanding your own capabilities and that of others is an essential part of leadership and your own journey through life. I have no doubt you will return to this book time and again.'

– Floyd Woodrow MBE DCM

'Sustaining resilience is something that most leaders would say you learn through experience; unfortunately experience is one of those things you acquire over time but find you needed it most a long time before you got it.

'This book cannot give you the experience, but it goes a long way in helping the reader understand what is happening or will happen to themselves and others around them, thereby helping them cope less stressfully with first time situations they encounter when placing their foot on the first and subsequent rungs of the leadership ladder. In today's world of high pace and disruptive technologies, leaders should remember that when they think they have made it on this topic, they should think again, or they will find themselves *past it*.'

– Graham Caleb, Co-Founder and CEO, PraXec Limited

'In this warm, human, practical and empathetic book, Julia Steward explores 'the close link between resilience and being comfortable with ourselves as individuals inhabiting the leadership role'. She focuses on our capacity to develop emotional resilience, exploring the relevant research but grounding her advice in the reality of leaders' everyday experiences and challenges. Julia suggests that emotional resilience may develop over time with experience and growing confidence, but that it is too important to be left to chance. She raises our awareness of how we can be more systematic and strategic about developing the strength to do a good job while safeguarding our physical and mental health and wellbeing. If leaders look after themselves, they will be better able to function successfully in their roles and support the wellbeing of those with whom and through whom they work. This book will help leaders at all levels, with all degrees of experience, negotiate this difficult but important challenge.'

– Jill Berry, an Ambassador for Leadership Matters and Associate for the National College for Teaching and Leadership

'This is not just a 'must read' but a 'must have' for all of us who find ourselves in leadership roles. You will find yourself returning to it again and again. In a beautifully written and illustrated practical guide to developing resilience, Julia pulls together many of the strands of research that have been published over the years and uses her considerable personal and professional experience to craft these into easily-understood advice. She has the capacity to step into our shoes and her humanity threads through every vignette. I found myself believing in the difference it would make to our world if every leader were to embrace the guidance in these pages.'

– Jan Evans, Managing Director, RSAdmissions Limited

'Thank you so much for the privilege of reading your book – I have already learned a great deal from it and found it very very helpful. Your work should be a great asset to a generation of teachers and leaders.'

– Ed Gregory, Headteacher, Bishop Henderson Church of England Primary School, Somerset

Acknowledgements

We live life forwards and understand it backwards. When I reflect on the twists and turns in life, I find it impossible to trace a direct path that has led to the creation of this book. If I had taken a different path at any moment in its history, I may not have ended up here. I have worked with many school leaders over the years and I have been privileged to be allowed a window into their world, often being inspired by their commitment and skill. References to individuals in the context of coaching are based on composite characters that reflect the generality of my coaching encounters.

So many people have opened doors for me on this journey that I cannot name them all. If you have ever shown interest in my writing or in its subject; attended a workshop I have run; listened as a member of an audience when I have spoken about resilience; or shared your feelings of inadequacy as a leader, you have also fuelled my determination to reach this point. I hope you will accept this acknowledgement as thanks for your part in my learning. I also acknowledge with gratitude the unique contribution of those without whose support the book in its current form would not exist.

Alex Sharratt at John Catt Educational grasped the project enthusiastically with both hands; he and his team have made it happen in an impressively short timescale. Jill Berry played a small but significant part in facilitating our connection. Tom Whittingham gave me a forum to explore the concept of emotional resilience for school leadership nine years ago: my early writing was prompted by the learning conversations that he gave me the space to facilitate. Chris Bryan at the University of St Mark and St John nurtured me through my MEd and Sean MacBlain, as external examiner, encouraged me to publish an academic paper based on my dissertation. I could not have found an illustrator more skilled at tuning into my thinking than Karen. Her artistry demonstrates that a picture really is worth a thousand words. Working with her has been a joy.

One of the benefits of writing a book like this is that it prompts many encounters with other people's writing, and conversations that have helped me to clarify my own thinking. Many such conversations with Gill Fowler have given me greater confidence in my work and helped me to clear a path for my writing. She, Julia Vaughan Smith, Jamie Stewart and, my son, Tom provided valuable feedback on sections of the book.

A book is a very insignificant legacy when compared to that which we give to the world as parents and grandparents. Through this work I have come to recognise the contribution of my close family to my own emotional resilience. Jan, Tom, James, Lucy, Ruth, Martha and Imogen have, in one way or another, helped me to keep in proportion life's challenges and setbacks. Whatever happens, their presence reminds me what really matters.

Contents

List of Exercises

Introduction

Why this book?

It is 1999 and in a spacious room in a West Country hotel, 12 headteachers are discussing leadership and how they feel about their job. It is the second day of a three-day national residential leadership programme. Trust is developing quickly amongst the group. It is rare for these leaders to be able to take time out of school and share the highs and lows of headship in a non-judgemental environment. 'To be honest,' says one, 'I'm waiting to be found out. I think one day someone's going to come and put a hand on my shoulder and tell me to move over and make way for someone who can really do the job'. 'I know,' says another, 'and it doesn't help when you go to county meetings and everyone else seems to be on top of the latest requirements, while I'm still wondering what they are.'

The dialogue is an approximation, but the scenario is real enough. As a facilitator of a national leadership programme for experienced headteachers, I noticed how frequently competent and apparently confident headteachers admitted to their fear of being 'found out'. Members of one group after another shared the same sense of inadequacy (even though the evidence of the programme showed them to be anything but inadequate). Along with the fear of being found out, it seemed, was a twin fear of anyone finding out that they worried about being found out. Undoubtedly, leaders need to display confidence if they expect people to follow them. It seemed here that a conspiracy of silence prevented them from sharing their fear even with close colleagues. The fear was compounded by a sense of isolation: each one imagined everyone else was feeling supremely confident. As they realised they were not the only ones, nervous laughter was followed by a palpable sense of relief. I wondered how much energy was being drained by the effort of keeping their vulnerability hidden, what the unconscious impact of their fear of being found out might be, and how their leadership was affected.

Thus began my journey of exploration into sustaining resilience for leadership. Through many group and one-to-one interactions with leaders, as well as through my own efforts at leadership, I have learned the truth of Warren Bennis's view:

'The process of becoming a leader is much the same as the process of becoming an integrated human being ... leadership is a metaphor for centeredness, congruity and balance in one's life.'[1]

In talking about the 'process' of becoming an integrated human being, and in referring to 'integration', Bennis is recognising a universal human truth: if we are to engage with the world with our whole selves, hiding nothing and holding nothing back, there is a journey to be undertaken. As we climb the leadership ladder, we need also to be paying attention to integrating within us the manifold manifestations of 'I'. 'I' am now an adult, a sister, a daughter, a mother, a friend, a mother-in-law, a grandmother and a leader. Different aspects of my character may show more or less in different situations; some I am comfortable to own and others that I wish I did not display. If I were to ask what happened to the child I once was, I have to acknowledge that she also remains somewhere within me. Some of the behaviours or beliefs I was taught as a child I have disregarded as an adult, because I have found them to be untrue or unhelpful. Others have become so much part of me that I do not even notice them or where they come from.

All families have their own culture – an unwritten set of rules and expectations that we absorb as children. My family culture was one where we were organised, and left little to chance. I learned to hide my 'free' self because it did not fit. I learned to love myself when I was organised, because that was a characteristic valued by my family. While I did not

---

1   Bennis, W. & Goldsmith, J. (1997): *Learning to Lead*. London: Nicholas Brealey.

consciously project to the world someone who was well organised, I was pleased when others recognised my organisational skills. When working with those who did not share those skills, I found it difficult to understand how they could be so disorganised. So much of my identity was wrapped up in being organised, that it was difficult to accept my own behaviour if, for example, I was running late for something. I was so convinced that I would be 'unlovable' if people knew I had mismanaged my time, that I preferred to pretend I had been delayed by heavy traffic rather than confess that I had left later than intended.

It is these 'split off' and unacceptable parts of ourselves that we need to embrace if we are to become 'integrated human beings'. Integrity in leadership is essential: it builds trust. True integrity can be achieved only when we can choose our own beliefs, values and behaviours, irrespective of the judgements we believe others are making about us. Once we are sufficiently confident to accept ourselves as we really are, we will not need to drain our energy by maintaining the shield that protects us from 'being found out'. Being able to accept ourselves allows us to interact more openly with others, improves our confidence, reduces stress and builds resilience.

'Resilience' or 'resiliency' is a term that is increasingly appearing in everyday language and in the literature of many disciplines. It is applied to engineering (in resilient materials), the planet (the resilience of the ecosystem), information technology systems (that are able to withstand attack) and organisations (that weather financial storms). When applied to people, resilience may be applied to physical or mental capacity and usually refers to an individual's ability to recover from some sort of setback, or to keep going in the face of adversity or challenge. About a decade after the experience described at the opening of this book, I was given an opportunity to lead some learning conversations with a focus on 'becoming ourselves as leaders'. I became aware of the close link between resilience and being comfortable with ourselves as individuals inhabiting the leadership role. Through discussions, reading and research, it has become evident that resilience of mind and resilience of body cannot be separated. In leadership we are preoccupied with planning, complex problem solving and steering the organisations we lead through change, often seeking increased efficiency and effectiveness. All these preoccupations demand intellectual engagement and creativity that exercise the mind. Many of us are so engrossed with what is going on in our heads that we pay little or no attention to the body that dutifully carries around our head day in, day out. Schools work hard to ensure that the 'learning environment' is as good as it can be. The building has to be welcoming and attractive; classrooms are inadequate if used only as spaces in which to teach: walls should display messages that reinforce learning. Whatever sphere of leadership we operate in, however attractive our office, the space we often neglect to evaluate is the space we occupy regardless of our changing environment: we inhabit our bodies first and we need to stop taking them for granted if we are to remain resilient. According to Boyatzis, 'sustained effective leadership will be adversely affected by the power-stress aroused in the process of fulfilling the leadership role.'[2] We may notice physical manifestations of stress if we choose to review our personal operating system.

Resilience, all things considered, is a combination of physical and mental strength. In *Man's Search for Meaning*[3], Victor Frankl writes of his experiences in the Nazi death camp at Auschwitz: 'When we are no longer able to change a situation, we are challenged to change ourselves.'

Reflecting on her resilience, a friend who had been diagnosed with cancer underlined the importance of being able to choose how we respond to events.

'I have learned – your mind can take you to places you don't want to go, and you don't have a lot of control over it. And that's when your emotional resilience just goes ... you can only have resilience if you're in a place where you've got a choice, when you're in those darkest hours and darkest places, you don't have a choice. Your mind has taken you there and you'd give anything not to be there.'

What she is describing here is the impact of fear. Though we interpret and describe them cognitively, emotions are physical manifestations of our body's reactions to external stimuli. Emotions are mediated by reason. As we mature, as people and as leaders, we learn not to 'overreact' to our feelings. For the most part, we avoid antagonistic behaviour, or

2   Boyatzis, R. E. (2006): An overview of intentional change from a complexity perspective. *Journal of Management Development*, 26 (7), 607-623.
3   Frankl, V. E. (2004): *Man's Search for Meaning*. London: Ebury Press, Random House.

being paralysed by fear, or crying when it seems inappropriate to do so. At best we consciously control our emotions and allow them to surface when the time is right. When we are conscious and accepting of our emotions, we can experience them safely.

It is when we are unaware of our emotional response to a situation that we can become overwhelmed, lose our way and behave in ways that divert us from our preferred direction of travel. My focus, therefore, is on **emotional** resilience and it is that to which I refer when I use the term 'resilience', unless I specify otherwise. Although I have acknowledged that physical, mental and emotional resilience are linked, it is when our emotions buckle under pressure that we lose the ability to take control of our responses.

Edward Lorenz, meteorologist and professor at the Massachusetts Institute of Technology, famously coined the term 'the butterfly effect'. It was originally applied to changes in weather, but has become a way of referring to the impact of small changes that have an effect beyond their apparent area of influence. Many years previously, in the 16th century, the English poet John Donne wrote 'No man is an island'. He also recognised the 'interconnectedness' of humanity. Each of us exists within a wider system that we influence and are influenced by. The first system each of us encounters is our family system. Whatever our working context, that context exists within a wider system, which influences our working practices. The headteachers that I refer to at the opening of this book were working in the maintained school system in the United Kingdom. Most of the examples I use in this book come from the education system, because that is the context in which I have been working for the last 20 years or so. I also stand outside that system, in that I have never been a teacher. Many of the examples I use and all the exercises I offer apply equally to all leadership. I hope this book will help you as a leader to be more aware of the influence of the system on your own working practice, as well as giving you a greater understanding of your own response to the context in which you work.

There are some pointers in this book and some exercises that will help you to understand how to support your own resilience. Regretfully, there are no quick fixes, but there is an opportunity to increase self-awareness if you can find time to reflect on your own behaviour. Sustaining resilience demands increasing the habits that support our resilience and changing those that undermine it. Try wearing your watch on a different wrist for a day, and notice how often you look where it used to be when you check the time. Changing habits takes time and commitment. If you walk the journey with support, you will almost certainly find it easier. I know from experience, however, that even seeking support takes many leaders to a place of vulnerability that is too difficult to contemplate. If you are one of those, I offer you this book as a means of opening the door to a different way of operating which may also allow you to accept help in the future.

The book is based on my experience of working with, quite literally, hundreds of leaders, most of who have been working in schools, along with insights from my academic research, reading, and my own experiences of life and leadership. I offer exercises that have proved helpful to those who have attended my workshops, suggestions for further exploration and questions, which are intended to prompt further thinking.

The framework for the book stems from the academic research I undertook when working towards a Master's degree in Education. I concluded that there are a number of factors that impact on our emotional resilience, which I define as 'the ability to remain on course and sustain emotional connection without being overwhelmed'.

A key driver of emotional resilience is our wellbeing. The better we feel, the more resilient we are, and the more resilient we are, the better we feel, so emotional resilience and wellbeing are mutually supportive. A sense of wellbeing is served by looking after our physical and mental health. We need to ensure we sleep, eat healthily, take exercise, keep personal and work commitments in reasonable balance and so on. If we manage all those things, our energy levels will be sustained. Greater energy can lead to higher productivity, but it is possible to use our energy fruitlessly, for example in worrying about things that we cannot change, or focusing on activities that do not lead to the outcomes we seek. Energy alone is not enough; we also need the ability to take control and act in our own best interests: a sense of agency. Our sense of agency is what allows us to take responsibility for our actions and it stems from our belief in our ability to make our own decisions and take actions that influence the course of events in the outside world. The stronger our sense of agency, the more able we are to distinguish our own inner voice from the demands of the 'oughts' and 'shoulds' that others impose on us. One of the decisions we may make if acting in our best interests, is to look after our wellbeing (rather than to sacrifice it for the sake of the organisation). Our ability to consciously take control of what is in our best long-term interest is also necessary for sustaining our emotional resilience. It sounds straightforward and logical, and yet many school leaders I have worked with find themselves too busy to focus on their own wellbeing. While they understand the theory and acknowledge the need, they find it difficult to make such behaviour habitual.

We need to look further. We need to explore leaders' internal dialogue, which is influenced by their core beliefs, values and habitual patterns of thinking, as well as the expectations imposed on them by the education system, as represented below.

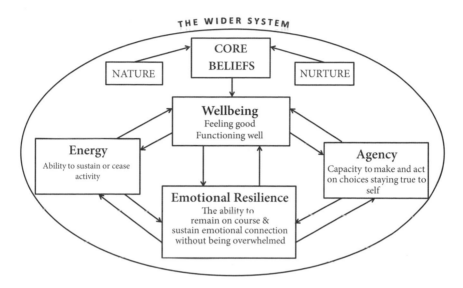

Figure 1: Factors interacting to affect leaders' emotional resilience

Using this book as a resource

The model becomes the framework for this book. I know that leaders generally have little time for reading, so I encourage you to start with whatever aspect seems to call to you. I hope it is something you will come back to, as different areas resonate at different times. The 'worth remembering' summaries at the end of each chapter are designed to help you to skim read if you wish to, or as a reminder if you go back to the same chapter sometime after your first reading. While all the chapters are interconnected, it is possible to explore one aspect and ignore the others. Exercises, designed to support you to reflect on ways in which you can develop more helpful habits to sustain your resilience, are given throughout. For those who wish to explore in greater depth, references and suggestions for further exploration are given at the end of the book.

Chapter One:
Why Emotional Resilience?

'Resilience matters and can be influenced. Everyone is bound to face shocks and setbacks at some point in life. But what makes the difference is how well we cope with these shocks, how well we bounce back ... Resilience – and psychological fitness in a broader sense – can also be learned and enhanced.'[4]

At about the time of the publication of the Young Foundation's report quoted above, I am in discussion with a group of Australian headteachers who are visiting a colleague. We are talking about the importance of resilience in school leadership. They all agree it is absolutely fundamental. 'So how do you develop it?' I ask. They hedge, as though the idea of proactively developing resilience has not occurred to them. 'It comes with experience,' they suggest. 'You make your mistakes in your first headship, take the learning and move on. It's tough at first, but gradually 'you learn that you can cope'. Not for the first time, I wonder if gaining the battle scars of a first headship is a rite of passage, to be worn as a veteran's medal, and whether it is appropriate to leave to chance the development of such a vital leadership attribute in a role which has the potential to shape the future of society.

---

4   The Young Foundation. (2009): *Sinking and Swimming: Britain's Unmet Needs*. London: The Young Foundation.

My opportunity to undertake systematic formal research to find out more came about almost by accident. I had been recruited as a university college tutor on a Master's programme in Education. It was suggested that I would be a better tutor if I had gone through the process myself and I shall be eternally grateful for that; I should never have become so steeped in the subject without such an incentive.

My first step was to carry out a survey of school leaders. Out of 49 respondents, 48 rated emotional resilience as 'very important', while less than a third were able to identify specific strategies that they use to maintain their own resilience. Anyone who holds a similar belief to the Australian leaders mentioned above – that resilience is something that develops as a result of experience – must simply wait until they happen upon the experiences that will build their resilience. On more than one occasion, I have had to tell someone who had been studying for a national professional qualification that they had not met the standard. If your first experience of failure happens when you are in your late 30s, studying for a professional qualification required to practice in your chosen profession, you will have had no practice at failing. Those who had only ever experienced success in life found it very difficult to accept that on this one occasion, they had failed. Our experience shapes how we see ourselves. When we are faced with information that challenges our self-image, we have the choice of adjusting our self-image, or keeping it intact and questioning the veracity of an assessor's decision. Those whose sense of identity depends upon their habit of success will find it difficult to make room for the concept of failure.

The word 'resilience' as an aspect of personal and professional development has been a topic of increasing interest since the early '70s. It is now widely accepted amongst psychologists that some, if not all, of the so-called 'protective factors' that improve resilience can be learned. The School of Positive Psychology at the University of Pennsylvania has been a driving force for much of the work that focuses on growing resilience. The Penn Resilience Programme (PRP), delivered to students to help them to deal with difficulties common in adolescence, is one of the most widely researched intervention programmes designed to combat depression in young people. With other approaches, the PRP underpins the US Army's Master Resilience Training (MRT), which has been running since 2009.

Peak physical fitness has always been at the heart of training for the armed services; a review of the content of the modules of the MRT shows clearly that the aim is to ensure the army is equally psychologically fit[5]. The majority of the programme is underpinned by Albert Ellis's adversity-belief-consequence (ABC) model, used in cognitive behaviour therapy, which rests on the notion that our beliefs about a particular situation drive our emotions and behaviour: change the belief and you change the behaviour.

The work of Martin Seligman on learned optimism[6] has built on that approach. It is not the adversity which damages our resilience, but our belief about its impact and our future in the light of that impact. In a systematic review of resilience training in the workplace from 2003 to 2014, Robertson et al[7] were unable to find definitive evidence of the most effective training content. However, their research does point to the benefit of including in any programme one-to-one support based on individual needs. In summary, it is evident that individuals and organisations can take a proactive approach to developing resilience.

None of us can avoid setbacks in life. I look on in awe as a friend who was diagnosed with cancer seems to embrace the diagnosis without resentment, fear, or anger, simply adjusting to the information and taking steps to ensure his end is as good as it can be. I feel impatient with another for whom a train cancellation prompts moaning and sighing far beyond what (to me) seems justified by the realisation that she will arrive home 30 minutes later than originally planned. Each of us faces challenges in life, and the degree to which any of us is challenged by a particular set of circumstances depends on the people we are: I was loved and accepted as a child while you were abandoned; I grew up thinking the world owes me a living but you grew up thinking you owe your life to the world. All of those experiences, our own sense of self and the challenges we meet every day, will have an impact on our resilience. The

5   Reivich, K. J., Seligman, M. E. P. & McBride, S. (2011): Master Resilience Training in the US Army. *American Psychologist*, 66 (1).

6   Seligman, M. (2006): *Learned Optimism* (Vintage ed.). New York, New York City: Vintage Books.

7   Robertson, I. T., Cooper, C. L., Sarkar, M. & Curran, T. (2015): Resilience training in the workplace from 2003 to 2014. *Journal of Occupational and Organizational Psychology*, pp. 533-562.

degree to which a particular situation is challenging is subjective.

A quick online search will provide a multitude of programmes designed to improve resilience in work situations. The mental health charity, Mind, offers training specifically for members of the emergency services; there is resilience training for professionals in the field of maternity healthcare; for those working with young people in health and social care; and for leaders in a variety of commercial organisations. A project known as BRiTE (Building Resilience in Teachers), funded by the Australian government, provides trainee, or pre-trainee teachers with the opportunity to engage in a five-module online programme to support their resilience. Programmes focused on the needs of school leaders are conspicuously absent.

All leaders have a degree of resilience. If they did not, they would be unable to carry out their role. My research suggests that many school leaders acknowledge the importance of resilience, but only about a third of those who were surveyed could identify measures that they took to foster their own resilience. We recognise the importance of regular servicing and refuelling for our cars and would hardly be surprised if, after several miles of driving with the fuel gauge on 'empty', the vehicle stopped functioning.

Many leaders forget to check their fuel gauge, and when they do, a reading of 'empty' all too often merely flags a challenge to see whether they can get to the next service station (weekend or holiday) without needing to stop. We take our bodies and minds for granted, and expect them to go on functioning effectively whether or not we take good care of them.

As consumers, we frequently put our lives into the hands of others, trusting in their training, competence and professionalism. I wonder how we would feel if we knew that the surgeon leading our complex operation, or the captain of the aeroplane flight we are taking across the Atlantic, was making potentially life or death decisions while sleep deprived, having not stopped for a proper meal for 24 hours, relying on excess coffee to get through the day. School leaders are not called on daily to make life or death decisions, but the decisions they make can and do make a difference to the education and life chances of hundreds of children and young people. If emotional resilience adds fuel to the journey, we cannot afford to leave its development to chance. To pay no attention to its maintenance is like ignoring the need to service and refuel your car and then wondering why it is not functioning at its best.

Inevitably, each of us will rate our own resilience according to our understanding of the term. However we view resilience, it is generally regarded as helpful in its capacity to allow us to keep going in the face of what life throws at us, and as helping us to withstand the effects of stress. Metaphors abound: a rubber band, for example, stretches to accommodate whatever it is being used to keep together; remove it, and it will regain its original shape. You can do this again and again and it will continue to flex and return to its original shape. Stretch it once too often, or too far, however, and it will eventually snap. When we consider psychological resilience, similar themes emerge. An advert for the US Army's Master Resilience Training (MRT) shows an egg being dropped and bouncing back as a tennis ball, accompanied by the words 'bounce, don't crack'. Individuals who are resilient do not break easily – the greater our resilience, the greater our capacity for regaining our shape and functioning effectively. It starts with our physiology, which underpins our functioning and our feeling. As an athlete, you may be more conscious of your physical than your mental resilience, but ask any top performer and they will tell you that given the same physical capacity, it is mental attitude that wins the race. As a leader, you may be more aware of your mental and emotional resilience than how physically resilient you are, but if you keep depriving your body of the things it needs for the brain to function effectively, such as water, food, sleep and exercise, you – or more likely, others – will begin to notice that you are losing your capacity to function. We talk about people 'acting out of character'. After too much stress, they cease to return to their original shape.

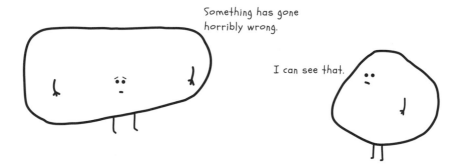

I have explored the concept of 'emotional resilience' with many leaders over the years. Each one has had a slightly different definition. One talked about the ability to deal with the knocks of life without being adversely affected in the long term; another felt it was an ability to deal with his emotional reaction to a situation so that it didn't have a negative impact on his behaviour; a third referred to withstanding 'the slings and arrows of outrageous fortune – what armoury you have' and another talked about 'emotional gymnastics'.

I focus on 'emotional' resilience because emotion is the link between physiology, feeling and thinking. Emotional resilience does not consist of not feeling, or showing, emotion; rather it is about having a proper respect for emotion. Acknowledging and accepting our emotions does not mean that they are always on show. Emotional resilience is a measure of the degree to which we can experience our emotions without them having a negative impact on our agenda.

'What we'd like you to do,' said my colleague and co-facilitator, 'is to decide who you'd like to work with over the coming year, sort yourselves into groups of four or five, and when you have made your decision, write the names of groups on the board and let us know you're ready for us to continue.' We left the room, as we thought, leaving the headteachers space to make their own decisions, unencumbered by the external pressures which we perceived they might feel if they were being watched by the group leaders. The minutes ticked by and we began to wonder whether we had made our directions sufficiently clear. Finally, we were invited back into the room. The atmosphere was tense and one of the headteachers was looking tearful. What was revealed in subsequent discussions was the high level of anxiety that our brief had caused.

We had made the assumption that those we were working with would find it fairly easy to follow the brief we had set. After all, we reasoned, they were all leaders in their own right, running complex organisations and used to making difficult decisions every day. With the benefit of hindsight I can understand what a difficult situation we had unwittingly created. At that time, I was unaware of how easily – in the timeless unconscious – we can be catapulted back into childhood. All the fears and insecurities we had then can be triggered in an instant. While some in the group saw our intention clearly and were happy to get on with the job in hand, others found themselves taken back to a playground where they feared no one wanted to play with them; or they were standing in a line on the sports field, knowing that they would be the last to be picked for the team. As is common in such situations, none of those who were feeling anxious was able to articulate exactly what was going on for them.

Anxiety undermines our ability to step outside our immediate emotional experience, recognise it for what it is, and take control. In this situation, their emotion overwhelmed their ability to apply reason. During our subsequent discussion, one of the facilitators commented on the similarity between childhood experience and what we were expecting of them now. Several of them then recognised the source of their anxiety; having done so, they could hand back the emotion to the child to whom it belonged.

Resilience in schools

Resilience is achieving increasing attention in schools, most often as a means of supporting students. Character education is already on the curriculum of schools in the UK and elsewhere; in 2016 the UK government endorsed its usefulness by reportedly setting aside £6m to further its development. Many headteachers, like those mentioned above, tell me that resilience grows through experience. I have never been a headteacher, but I think of it as being a little like having your first child. The emotional pressure, which comes from the knowledge that suddenly you are responsible for another human being's life, can feel overwhelming at times. By the time you have your second child, you can relax a little, knowing that you have managed reasonably well to look after the first. (Until you discover that all children – like all schools – are different.) The first year in headship is undoubtedly the most challenging, and as the school cycle repeats itself, year on year, the number of things which you have not dealt with previously reduces, and you may even come to believe that you can do the job effectively. The outcome of the survey I carried out as part of my research suggests that there may be a moment when the scales begin to tip back towards a lack of confidence. Responses to the survey revealed that the headteachers who had been in the job the longest were more likely to agree with the statement 'I worry I'm not good enough'. Those who have offered an explanation for this apparent regression in confidence have suggested that more is expected of those who have been longer in post (they have less right to fail, apparently, and are less likely to ask for help) and/or that they have less energy and worry about being shown up by more energetic potential successors.

It is often said that nothing prepares you for your first headship. However, there are things you can do to build your resilience. You would be unlikely to run a marathon without going into training first and if you did, it would certainly be a great deal more challenging than it would be if you had taken care to develop your fitness first. Yet individuals are now able to take on the role of headteacher with no formal training at all. Even when the National Professional Qualification for Headship (NPQH) was mandatory for first-time headteachers, little attention was paid to how to develop resilience. The competency 'resilience and emotional maturity' was tested in later versions of the qualification and yet there is little, if any, attempt to design interventions that specifically support resilience.

The intentional change model[8] by Boyatzis talks about 'discontinuities' or 'discoveries', which lead to a desire to change. Something has to make us stop and question whether there is another way. The trouble is, like A. A. Milne's Winnie the Pooh, who habitually arrives downstairs by being trailed by one leg behind Christopher Robin 'bump, bump, bump' on the back of his head, we are often far too busy 'bumping' to stop and consider

---

8   Boyatzis, R. E. (2006): An overview of intentional change from a complexity perspective. *Journal of Management Development*, 26 (7), 607-623.

whether things could be different. Sometimes the only thing that makes us stop and question our habitual behaviour is a sort of crisis or threat.

It is 2006. In Derbyshire a new headteacher is appointed to the largest primary school in the county. With 500 pupils on roll, it is set to expand further over the next couple of years to become one of the largest in the country. School funding is allocated based on the number of pupils on roll in the previous year. Additional pupils who arrive mid-year are funded only retrospectively. Rapid expansion puts a particular strain on the system and leads to a deficit budget, necessitating redundancies. Morale dips. Expansion means new buildings. New buildings mean disruption on the site. The headteacher, in addition to attempting to lift morale, is required to ensure that all runs smoothly with the building, juggling that responsibility with the day-to-day management of the school and ensuring the strategic educational plan remains in focus. Additional pressure means longer hours, which demands giving up outside pursuits and investing more and more energy in the school. Rapid expansion means routines are less well embedded and some children's behaviour is particularly challenging. The headteacher's workload increases, as he is now called on to provide backup when a child's behaviour is out of control. He is seen less by colleagues outside of school. He notices that his childhood stammer has returned and he is unable to fulfil duties involving public speaking. A good night's sleep is a distant memory and he finds himself increasingly tearful. Finally he has to acknowledge his distress. The job has overwhelmed him.

James Hilton, the headteacher appointed to that Derbyshire school, tells his story in *Leading from the Edge*[9]. It is an account that echoes many of the stories I have heard from leaders I have worked with in a confidential environment. In the everyday busy-ness of headship he ignored the physical warning signs of the stress he was experiencing. Only in retrospect was he able to identify that the back pain, migraines, shortness of breath, chest pains, stammer and other symptoms were all manifestations of 'a mind and body that had spent too much time in 'fight or flight' mode'.

Being unaware of the need to change can be attributed to what Boyatzis sees as the human psyche's inclination to protect itself from the

---

9   Hilton, J. (2016): *Leading from the Edge*. London and New York: Bloomsbury Publishing.

consciousness of the totality of information about ourselves[10]. It is an ego-defence mechanism that serves to protect us, but it can also hijack our best intentions if we are blind to unhelpful habits of thinking and behaviour. As we rush from one task to another, busy doing rather than being, there is a danger that we become the proverbial 'boiling frogs' which, as the story goes, react swiftly if put into a pot of boiling water by jumping out. If they are put in cool water and the heat gradually increased, however, then they will be unaware of the temperature change and boil to death.

Boyatzis talks about intentional change as being discontinuous, usually in response to an epiphany moment; the frog being put into hot water, if you like. The greater the impact, the greater the motivation to change: something small in itself may turn out to be the tipping point. For school leaders, one too many demanding parents, feeling humiliated in public,

---

10   Boyatzis, R. E. (2006): An overview of intentional change from a complexity perspective. *Journal of Management Development*, 26 (7), 607-623.

a period of enforced absence from school through illness – any of these can trigger a realisation that the job, and indeed life, has, apparently suddenly, become too much to cope with. Reviewing this type of experience with those I have coached confirms that we live life forwards, but understand it backwards. Clients relate their history as someone who has been acting in a drama without knowing the script of the final episode. It is only after the final credits that they can see the significance of events and conversations that contributed to the outcome that they are now living with.

None of us knows how resilient we are until we are tested. History is full of individuals who have triumphed against the odds and kept going in the face of, apparently, hopelessly insurmountable challenges. Nelson Mandella, Brian Keenan, Terry Waite, all experienced profoundly testing experiences in captivity and yet kept going; they didn't just give up, or go mad. These examples illustrate the extremes, and those involved were well aware that they were being tested. We are much more likely to be faced with the type of testing times illustrated by the boiling frog story. The increase in pressure is so gradual that we are disinclined even to notice the change. We tell ourselves that we 'ought to be able to cope', which adds to the burden that we are carrying, making it harder to ask for help because we see it as a sign of weakness. Most of us know from experience that events that trigger an unhelpful emotional response when we are having a bad day are without significant impact on a good day. When our emotional resilience is high, we can cope with challenges that would derail us when we are feeling fragile.

A close colleague going through a difficult divorce came to me one day: 'I need to share this with you,' she said. 'Can you watch me, please? I'm under quite a lot of pressure at home at the moment, and I don't want to end up doing something silly at work as a result.'

We all need someone at work with whom we can have that conversation, someone to whom we give permission to say 'you're getting it wrong'. I know that is not easy in schools. I have had many conversations with deputy headteachers sharing concerns about their headteachers. The majority have backed off having the difficult conversation with their boss because 'at the end of the day s/he is going to give me a reference and I don't want to rock the boat'. I was heartened by a conversation with a staff governor who told me that his headteacher had recommended he become a governor because he was 'not afraid to challenge her in public'. Such a relationship takes time to develop and can only flourish in a climate of trust. A headteacher who does not trust him or herself in the role is unlikely to trust others sufficiently to be open to challenge.

Leadership is stressful. It demands decisions that have far-reaching consequences, many of which may be only half-known to its practitioners. To fulfil their role successfully, leaders require a degree of self-management seldom required in other roles. When mistakes are made, they are very visible. Making mistakes is, in many ways, the business of schools, in that they are places of learning; no one can learn without encountering failure and feeling vulnerable. If you have ever sat in a meeting, assuming that you are the only person who does not have complete clarity concerning what is being expected, only to find afterwards that you have asked the very question that everyone else wanted to ask, you will understand the challenges of learning in public.

Learning makes us vulnerable: we must be humble, curious and ready to accept that we do not know. Staff and students have to be prepared to fail and even if the adults are able to manage their emotions, many or most of the pupils (depending on their maturity) will not have mastered this technique. All leaders must engage emotionally with their followers if they are to win hearts and minds. In schools, this means interacting not only with staff, but also with parents and children. The *dramatis personae* in a school replicate that in a family. Adults act *in loco parentis* and yet the adults in school (who play the role of step-parents in the system) are not always in agreement with the birth parent. The actual birth parents may or may not still have total responsibility for their children. In addition, many school leaders will tell you that they frequently act as counsellors to parents, staff and children. These emotional demands are compounded when leaders also find themselves having to compromise their own values in order to meet the demands of the wider system. This may be excluding a pupil when all attempts to keep him or her in school have failed; it may mean fining parents whose own lives are chaotic, because they have not ensured their children attend school regularly, or investing the school budget in adapting accommodation to allow for the introduction of universal free school meals, when only a small minority of the community will benefit.

John West-Burnham[11] describes each interaction as being 'based on perception rather than logic and rationality – or, at least in competing rationalities'. He describes the inner life of school leaders as being like a reservoir that needs constant refilling if it is not to run dry at the very moment when the floodgates need to be open as 'energy, compassion, creativity, optimism, courage and hope are called on. The deeper the reservoir the more can be given, but eventually even the deepest reservoir will begin to run low'.

Having ultimate public accountability for results whose foundations are laid before – in some cases long before – children cross the threshold of their school is the white noise that all school leaders live with. For some, it is a constant pressure. Like the headteachers I met on the leadership programme I wrote about at the start of this book, they are 'waiting to be found out'. Others have learned to live with the pressures of public accountability, seeing themselves as accountable first to the students and their parents, confident to adjust their priorities in accordance with the context of the school, and prepared to live with the risk of others' judgement that they are not good enough.

For many, challenge is part of the attraction of the role. Like the White Queen in *Alice through the Looking Glass* this may mean believing 'as many as six impossible things before breakfast'. Optimism is essential, for when a leader loses hope, so does the community. Sometimes this will mean hiding one's true feelings in order to inspire confidence in others. There is an element of acting in front of an audience in leadership (and some would say, in teaching, too). In response to a question 'who are you when you're not being a headteacher?' one interviewee described his propensity for practical jokes and responded 'I guess I'm more grown up when I'm being a headteacher'. Another commented 'I am who I am' and a third described herself as a totally different character in headship.

Leaders may make the emotional weather of their organisation but to be successful they must be authentic. Acting a role for a purpose will take them so far, but to live permanently with pretence is exhausting. If they (albeit unconsciously) hide their own true feelings, even from themselves, they will be found out: their true feelings will emerge. In his

---

11   West-Burnham, J. (2009): *Rethinking Educational Leadership*. London: Continuum International Publishing Group.

book *Learned Optimism,* Martin Seligman refers to 'realistic optimism'.[12] To go out without a coat, smiling and telling everyone that the sun is shining when everyone can see that the storm clouds are gathering, will only undermine people's confidence in your judgement.

Phrases that embody the concept of 'every pupil achieving their full potential' proliferate on school websites. If this is the work of a school leader, success is impossible to measure. The government may have expectations of pupils' academic ability at particular stages of development, but the truth is that none of us knows the limits of our own ability. How will I ever know whether I have reached my 'full potential' when each day brings new challenges, new tests of character and new opportunities to grow? If schools are places of learning, we might legitimately define a successful leader as one who models learning and creates a climate where failure is seen as acceptable: a step on the road to success. More than ever before, schools are required to be learning organisations with practitioners who learn from one another and use research to guide their thinking and actions. No one can learn if they are afraid of failure. Too many failures before achieving success, or indeed, ill-timed failures (just before the arrival of the schools' inspectorate, for example) and your school will be judged to have failed its students and its community. Being the person ultimately responsible for holding others to account while also encouraging them to take risks creates tension.

Unlike CEOs of large organisations who are generally not known to their customers, headteachers of schools are often seen as synonymous with the school. Indeed many school leaders I have come across find it difficult to separate their own identity from that of their school. Sitting in the audience of a conference several years ago, where a headteacher was sharing his school's journey to convert to an academy, I was struck by his opening statement. 'I am an outstanding school'. More frequently I have heard 'we are an outstanding school' but rarely 'the school I lead has been judged outstanding'. If the school 'fails' then the headteacher has failed. The only person not allowed to fail in this learning organisation is the person responsible for holding others to account.

---

12   Seligman, M. (2006): *Learned Optimism* (Vintage ed.). New York, New York City: Vintage Books.

Headteachers must judge carefully the pace of change needed for success, for when it does not come quickly enough, responsibility for that failure is laid at the door of the individual ultimately accountable. Every day as a school leader, you will make decisions that balance conflicting needs of different stakeholders with generally positive outcomes. Many of these will cause you no discomfort, but some you will agonise over: when you are required to make a colleague redundant; when you have to acknowledge that a colleague who has given long and faithful service is no longer capable of fulfilling the requirements of the job; when you have to exclude a student; when you have to accept that you cannot meet the needs of a vulnerable pupil; when involving social services means the break-up of a family. Responding to human vulnerability and frailty consumes our emotional energy. If we do not take the trouble to refill our emotional reservoir, it will run dry, leaving us emotionally, mentally and physically exhausted. Our internal landscape becomes distorted making objective rational thought difficult as we blame ourselves for events that are beyond our control.

Of all the emotions, fear is perhaps the one that plays the greatest havoc with our capacity for rational thought. A 'life threatening' incident (whether the threat is to physical safety, or to one's personal or professional sense of identity) inevitably causes stress as adrenalin and cortisol flood through our bodies, preparing us for fight or flight. We act instinctively.

In his book Do No Harm: Stories of Life, Death and Brain Surgery[13] the neurosurgeon Henry Marsh talks about how he deliberately protects himself from the emotions that would naturally be triggered by cutting in to a human brain. This act of emotional distance allows him to do his job. As a medical student he allowed himself to feel sympathy for patients 'because I was not responsible for what happened to them,' he says. Having ultimate responsibility for the success or otherwise of an operation – no matter who had been involved – changed that, for 'with responsibility comes fear of failure'.

---

13   Marsh, H. (2014): *Do No Harm: Stories of Life, Death and Brain Surgery*. London: Weidenfeld & Nicolson.

As a leader, you work with and through others and are accountable for the success or otherwise of your operation, even though you may not be responsible for every action that led to the outcome. You are dealing not only with your own emotions, but the emotions experienced by those you interact with. Communication comes relatively easily to most of us; we forget what a complex process it is. I speak, you listen; you speak, I listen. We understand each other. The truth is, however carefully we prepare our communications (and often we are too busy to do this carefully) we have no control over how they will be received. At best, leaders help to create the right emotional climate for everyone to flourish. School leaders have to manage their own emotions in order to lead effectively; they are faced every day with children and adolescents who have not yet learned to do so, as well as some adults who struggle to understand their own emotions and, consequently, manage them badly.

Unmanaged emotion can lead us to behave in ways that we later regret. All other things being equal, our emotional responses are mediated by our cognitive processes and/or by early conditioning and social convention. When confronted with difficult issues, however, we may not have the processing time we need to make a rational response, particularly if our own emotions are triggered. Thoughts and feelings are so closely linked, that sometimes it is difficult to distinguish one from the other. Our emotional reactions may stem from an underlying thought that we are not even conscious of. Comments that we hear as innocuous, or even helpful, from some individuals, sound critical when coming from the mouths of others whose motives we suspect in some way.

It is the year 2000 and I have just been appointed to the leadership of a large team of headteachers and ex-headteachers, all of whom are education professionals. I have never trained as a teacher and the first time anyone paid me to work in a school it was many years previously when I was an Ofsted lay inspector. I am unsettled by one member of the team who has the habit of holding up discussions of what seem to me pretty obvious solutions to problems. 'Can we just hold on a moment, go back, and consider what we are saying here?' is a frequent interjection. I struggle not to be defensive, feeling my competence is being questioned. As I look back now, I can see that my difficulty with hearing and giving weight to these early interventions was less about my impatience to move towards what I saw as an obvious solution, than my fear that my leadership was being called into question. I lacked confidence in the role and the comments by this colleague got straight through my defences. I learned to trust her motivation and she made it obvious that she trusted my leadership. Now I have grown in confidence and can generally deal with challenges from group members, but the truth is my defences can still be triggered when I am feeling tired, or anxious, or I have not yet established trust with the person raising the question. To be effective leaders in any field, we need to be able to manage our emotions and in order to manage them then we need to understand them. To be able to choose our behaviour, we must be aware of our emotional responses, and be able to manage the behaviour that they trigger. If resilience is about bouncing back in the face of difficulties with a sense of remaining on course, being emotionally resilient will make us more able to deal with the 'emotional wake' of an event. The water will be calmer; the waves smaller, and others on the sea are less likely to be affected.

Patterson and Kelleher's research, outlined in *Resilient School Leaders*[14] suggests that our ability to reflect on challenging experiences is what makes the difference between returning to the status quo, or emerging from adversity stronger than before. Even in places of learning, it is hard for leaders to find time to stop, reflect on and learn from their behaviour, while letting go of the recriminations. Many people tell me they reflect in the car on the homeward journey. That may help in the moment (if it does not detract from focusing on your driving) but real learning happens when you are able to review behaviour over time in order to recognise patterns. If you enjoy writing at length, you will benefit from a reflective diary. If that seems over burdensome, you may find the following format helpful.

It reflects feedback I received from a leader who found writing at length too much of a challenge. It shouldn't take more than 10-15 mins a week.

---

14   Patterson, J. L. & Kelleher, P. (2005): *Resilient School Leaders*. Alexandria, VA: Association for Supervision and Curriculum Development.

Exercise 1: Learning log

Columns 1 & 2: Date (week beginning) & 1-5 scale (5 high)		Things that went well	Things that didn't go well	Rating of resilience at the end of week
Example 5.1.18	5	Monday, ran staff meeting. Everyone positive & motivated.	Mis-managed time & ended up tired & irritable after working later than intended. Was grumpy about going to the in-laws.	4
etc				

As a school leader there will be times when you feel anger, frustration, sadness, fear and a whole host of other emotions. You may or may not choose to express those in the moment in which you feel them, but when you are overwhelmed by an emotion, you lose the capacity to choose. The more able you are to recognise and express your emotion, the less likely you are to lose the capacity to choose how and when you express it. Imagine you notice a colleague arriving late on several occasions. At first, you tell yourself it is an isolated incident. You notice again when you are in the middle of a conversation with a parent. Someone else tells you the colleague is going through a difficult time, so on the next occasion you observe lateness, you again excuse the behaviour to yourself.

Each time you let the behaviour pass, you are unconsciously becoming more irritated. Comes the morning when you are yourself running late because one of your own children was delayed by being unable to find his homework on the way to school, when all the traffic lights seemed to be on red on your journey to work, and when you arrive to find that your secretary has called in sick: at the end of your tether for all sorts of reasons not related to the colleague's lateness, you decide finally to confront the behaviour. Before you realise it, you are engaged in a tirade of criticism, which is not how you would have chosen to tackle the lateness. What started as mild irritation has become significant anger, and it has overtaken you. You have lost your capacity to choose.

Training and practice can make us more able to manage our emotions. Soldiers are put in threatening situations again and again in training, so that when an event happens on the battlefield, they do not need to think what to do. The frequent drilling they have gone through makes their response automatic. For the same reason, we carry out fire practices in schools, (the term 'fire-drill' seems to have fallen out of fashion) so that everyone knows exactly what to do: there is no place for panic or fear before the automatic behavioural response is prompted. It is often said that conscripts to an army are far more likely to flee in the face of battle than those who have been trained. Surely, the same must be true in other walks of life. Just as soldiers resist the temptation to run when they are fearful, so leaders have to overcome their instinctive emotional reaction if they are to stay the course.

Developing and sustaining emotional resilience

If 'the process of becoming a leader is much the same as the process of becoming an integrated human being'[15] then how do we learn leadership? We learn about life by living it. For most of us, wisdom and experience come with age. In life and in leadership, however, there are areas of focus that help to accelerate that learning. One thing we can do to accelerate our quest to become 'an integrated human being' is to learn about ourselves, and to be aware of things that undermine or support our own emotional resilience: the things that tax us and the things that energise us.

Below are two tables to help you to identify factors that are known to foster or undermine emotional resilience. Some suggestions are given: if they have an impact on you, please score them; if not, identify for yourself events or factors that affect your emotional resilience. In column A, score each on a 1-10 scale (10 is high).

In column B, score the same event according to its frequency. 10 would indicate that it is something that happens daily; 1 would be something that happens very infrequently. Some things, which on their own have

---

15   Bennis, W. & Goldsmith, J. (1997). *Learning to Lead*. London: Nicholas Brealey.

little impact, may build up over time if they happen frequently; others may happen infrequently, but have a bigger impact. In order to calculate the relative impact, for each event, multiply A x B to get the total for each event. To gain an indication of how much is in your resilience reservoir, follow the directions below the second table.

Exercise 2: Factors that sustain or undermine your emotional resilience

	Sustaining factor	A Impact score 1-10; 10 high	B Frequency score 1-10; 10 high	A x B
1	Support of family/friends			
2	Achieving success at work			
3	Evidence of having made a positive difference			
4	Time spent proactively relieving stress in a particular leisure activity			
5	The sense of a job well done			
6	Being in the fresh air			
7				
8				
9				
10				
			Total	

	Undermining factor	A Impact score 1-10; 10 high	B Frequency score 1-10; 10 high	A x B
1	Overwork			
2	Feeling ineffective			
3	Dealing with difficult colleagues			
4	Feeling taken for granted			
5	Being unclear about others' expectations			
6	Not having the time to do the job I'd like to do			
7	Feeling out of control			
8				
9				
10				
			Total	

When you have the total for the Sustaining Factors and the Undermining Factors, take the second from the first to check how much is in your emotional resilience reservoir.

After many years of coaching leaders, I am aware of some of the challenges that are common to many. As a leader your role will almost certainly include holding others accountable for their performance and behaviour. If you find it difficult to be clear when things are not going the way you would wish, you can rehearse your side of the dialogue (ideally with a partner) and practise using different strategies until you find one which works for you. If you find speaking to large groups a challenge, you can find ways to build up to that, starting with small groups and working up to larger ones. The more you practise, the more confident you are likely to become, but just as there are no dress rehearsals for life, neither are there for leadership. Leadership is about learning in public. The conductor of an orchestra can practise her craft only with an orchestra. A leader can rehearse dialogue in private, learn about the theory of leadership, but it is only when faced with the reality of leadership that she knows whether or not the rehearsals have been effective. One thing we can all do to prepare ourselves is to learn more about ourselves so that we recognise our own vulnerability and patterns of unhelpful behaviour, which accompany those feelings of vulnerability.

The contract for the Leadership Programme for Serving Headteachers has been re-let and I find myself working with a new provider covering a wider geographical region. We are all re-interviewed at the Hay Group offices in London and some of my colleagues have not been appointed to continue in their previous role. To my surprise and delight, I am assigned to the role of 'lead facilitator', which suggests I did well in the selection process and means I will have a responsibility for quality assuring the delivery and effectiveness of the team. I am aware that one of the lead facilitators from my previous team has not been selected to lead this time round, and I know she will be disappointed. Perhaps, I imagine, I have taken her place.

The programme has changed and the designers are keen to see it in practice. Another lead facilitator and I are working on the first delivery and someone from the Hay Group comes to observe. I have been observed several times previously without fear, but something about the fact that I see myself as having been 'elevated' to the role of 'lead' facilitator tells me that I cannot afford to get it wrong this time (whatever that means). Happily, I am facilitating a session that always goes well. But, something has changed; those in front of me look unreceptive and disengaged, and invitations to discuss with each other are met with blank stares. This was not what I was expecting. All I am aware of in the moment is fear of failure. With fear taking over, I strain to take control of the situation. I ask closed questions that limit (or kill) the participants' opportunity for discussion. I am now in a maze and cannot find the way out. I speak more and invite fewer contributions. The less engaged the participants, the more controlling I become. At the end of the session (not surprisingly, it finishes in record time with almost no space for discussion) my confidence in my ability to do the job expected of me has seeped out of my toes. I apologise to my co-facilitator and make for the toilet, unable to meet anyone's eye. In reflecting on the session afterwards I am able to identify what happened, and how my own unrealistic and inappropriate expectations of myself have hijacked me. On previous occasions I had been able to focus more on the needs of the group. It was when someone put that word 'lead' in front of the term 'facilitator' that I became unconsciously preoccupied with the need to prove myself as worthy of the term.

When we know ourselves well, recognise what triggers our emotions AND can guard against their being triggered in the moment (much more difficult) we are far less likely to become inappropriately overwhelmed by emotions: they no longer get in the way of our achieving our goal. However, to deny that those emotions exist, and to pretend that we do not feel, is to cut off part of ourselves, which is not helpful. If we want to bring our whole selves to all our endeavours, we need to be able to integrate what we may view as the good, the bad and the ugly within us. If I had not been aware of my fear of not being worthy of the title 'lead facilitator' and therefore needing to prove myself, I would not have understood what triggered the unhelpful behaviour in the example above, and I should have lost an opportunity to learn from the experience.

Belinda Harris talks about the importance of leaders displaying 'rigorous self honesty and soul searching and a willingness to befriend the multiple selves that constitute their personality ... to become intimately acquainted with the more neglected aspects of self, such as the vulnerable self that is hidden behind learned defences'.[16] Hiding our vulnerability undermines our authenticity and adds to our fear of 'being found out'.

Managing our emotions is different from numbing ourselves to their presence. Leaders need to understand themselves and their own insecurities, to accept them with self-compassion if they are to be truly authentic. Perhaps the hardest emotion to manage in leadership is the sense of vulnerability. While the traditional 'hero-leader' might be a character from the past, the

---

16   Harris, B. (2007): *Supporting the Emotional Work of School Leaders*. London: Paul Chapman.

school community requires a complex set of attributes from its leaders: they must be sufficiently vulnerable to be seen as human, but sufficiently invincible to be able to cope in the face of innumerable challenges. Understandably, most of us resist feeling pain or vulnerability. When we are aware that others are depending on us, as the community depends on its leader, it is even more important that we keep up the pretence. We find ways to take the edge off the pain, whether we do so consciously or not: it might be through comfort eating, or 'needing' a drink (as opposed to choosing to have one), through burying ourselves in work or over-exercising – anything that distracts us from the pain we are feeling.

Emotional self-awareness and emotional self-regulation are well documented as necessary for effective leadership. They are necessary for, but do not themselves lead to, emotional resilience. One may recognise and manage one's emotions, but the more energy that is consumed in doing so, the greater the capacity for exhaustion, and the less energy there is for creative activity. Emotional resilience requires a deep knowledge of self: not simply to recognise the emotions, but also to understand their origin and accept them without holding on to emotions that are destructive to the self. According to the psychotherapist Sheldon Kopp: 'all of the significant battles are waged within the self.' If we are to cultivate emotional resilience, we need to still the destructive internal battles so that we have more creative energy to engage with the battles in the outside world.

A recent systematic review of interventions designed to build and sustain resilience[17] found that most programmes use a cognitive behavioural approach to developing resilience: those undertaking the programme are encouraged to notice their thoughts and change those that prove unhelpful. Mindfulness meditation is increasingly being recommended in schools in the USA and the UK to improve the emotional wellbeing of students. It is also used in the management of pain. In essence, the practice is a means of training the brain to focus on the present, rather than allowing it unhelpfully to ruminate on the past, or involuntarily build up pictures of an undesirable future. Our minds are quite capable

---

17   Robertson, I. T., Cooper, C. L., Sarkar, M. & Curran, T. (2015): Resilience training in the workplace from 2003 to 2014. *Journal of Occupational and Organizational Psychology*, pp. 533-562.

of taking us to places where we experience anxiety and stress irrespective of external factors. Daniel Goleman[18] points to regular relaxation or meditation practice as being instrumental in reducing the inclination of the amygdala (sometimes called the brain's alarm bell) to respond to stress. Furthermore, when two groups of people were subjected to stressful experiences while their brains were scanned for brain activity, the group considered resilient to life's ups and downs showed a much quicker calming of the amygdala activity than the less resilient group.

Meditation practice, he maintains, somehow appears to re-calibrate the amygdala. 'This neural resetting gives us the ability to recover more quickly from amygdala hijacks, while making us less prone to them in the first place. The net result is that we are susceptible to distress less often and our bouts are shorter.' The practice of mindfulness or other forms of meditation – stilling, presence, focusing on the present moment, moves us from the practice of emotional intelligence – which might be seen as a set of competencies that can be learned and consciously pulled out of a toolkit at the right moment – to a different way of being which, with practice, becomes part of who we are. We are used to this idea of practice making perfect. In this case, we do not aim for perfection: it is the practice itself which is the end goal, and the moment we start thinking about how good we are at being ourselves, we lose focus on the importance on the practice for its own sake.

'You don't have to like it; you just have to do it' is a mantra that I have found myself using in several situations after hearing it first when I joined the eight-week mindfulness-based stress reduction (MBSR) course. I was persuaded to try it out when I heard a speaker from Guys and St Thomas's NHS Trust talking at a conference. He told the story of how the news of his success using mindfulness with his patients had encouraged several of his colleagues to send their patients to him. His list became so long that he was in danger of being overwhelmed with work and was becoming stressed. When a colleague suggested he should be doing the MBSR course, he was sceptical 'but that's for my patients' he said. 'Why would I need to do it?' The colleague persisted and he eventually undertook the course.

---

18 Goleman, D. (1988): *Working with Emotional Intelligence*. London: Bloomsbury.

To his amazement, it made a considerable difference not just to himself, but also to his patients – even those who were not themselves practising mindfulness. 'I can't explain it' he said. 'I am practising mindfulness and my patients are getting better.'

Some schools are now practising mindfulness with their students. Visiting one of these, I asked whether the practice extended to the senior leadership team. From the leader's reaction, it was clear that she had not even considered it as a possibility. When I visited the school where I was a governor, the importance of stopping and noticing was very much in my mind during a particular lunchtime. I noticed how teachers consumed lunch in record time (or did not stop to eat at all) then hurtled through corridors, picking up their coats as they went, as they rushed off to take lunchtime clubs. 'Lunchtimes are for wimps,' a headteacher at a friend's school stated, when she took on the role of business manager.

During a World Science Festival broadcast: *How We Bounce Back: The New Science of Human Resilience*[19], author and specialist in meditation, Matthieu Ricard points out that we are happy to spend years learning to read and write, play chess and music and so on, and yet we expect our mind to be optimal just because we want it to be so. He marvels that we should expect our mind to be balanced and compassionate without doing anything about it. As the scientific community finds scientific explanations for what Buddhist monks have experienced for generations, perhaps education will begin to take account of how we become 'integrated human beings' and offer the opportunity, not only to pupils, but also to adults who help to create the climate for learning in our schools.

Worth remembering

- Emotional resilience matters and can be influenced.
- It is not external factors which knock us off course, but how we respond to them.
- Regular time for reflection strengthens our capacity to learn from experience.
- Identifying things that support our resilience and practising them helps to ensure that we have resources in reserve when adversity strikes.
- You may become a boiling frog without noticing: give someone permission to tell you.

One of the ways to guard against becoming a boiling frog, or being knocked off course by external events is to ensure that we take care of our own health and wellbeing. For leaders, who are pre-occupied with the demands of the role (including, for some, the health and wellbeing of their workforce) that presents a challenge. It is one which they cannot afford to ignore if they are to continue to lead effectively.

---

19   World Science Festival. (17 February 2015): *How we bounce back: The new science of human resilience.* Available at: https://www.youtube.com/watch?v=XXRsQFDgnX8&t=6s [Accessed 18 February 2017].

Chapter Two:
Health and Wellbeing

If we want to be the author of our own destiny in life, taking care of our own health and wellbeing is essential.

'An individual's mental capital and mental wellbeing crucially affects their path through life. Moreover, [mental health and wellbeing] are vitally important for the healthy functioning of families, communities and society. Together, they fundamentally affect behaviour, social cohesion, social inclusion, and our prosperity.'[20]

The Foresight Mental Capital and Wellbeing Project report quoted here was commissioned by the government in order to inform public policy and ensure that UK citizens were in the best position to meet the challenges of the 21st century. Ten years later we are beginning to see changes in attitudes to mental health and wellbeing. Where once we consulted a doctor only if we felt ill, we are now invited to health checks of one sort or another, and we are given advice concerning how to look after our physical health. Attitudes to mental health are changing, as high profile individuals speak about their experience of depression, bipolar disorder and other forms of mental ill-health. The increasing incidence of dementia in old age has made many of us more aware of

---

20   Government Office for Science. (2008): *Mental Capital and Wellbeing Summary*. London: HMSO.

the importance of an active mind as well as an active body. Meanwhile, many of my clients are still so focused on getting their job done, that they have no time to stop and consider the link between physical and mental wellbeing: they run themselves into the ground in term time and rely on the school holiday to pay back the debt of over-use of their personal resources during the term. The first Director-General of the World Health Organization (WHO) was appointed in 1948 highlighted 'without mental health there can be no true physical health' and an editorial in the WHO Bulletin in 2013 underlines the proposition: 'The time has now come to do away with the artificial divisions between mental and physical health.'[21]

What is meant by wellbeing and how can it be influenced?

Research undertaken by the New Economics Foundation (NEF)[22] defines the concept of wellbeing very simply as:

- feeling good.
- functioning well.

There is no distinction here between mental and physical wellbeing. While many of us engage in work that is largely sedentary and cerebral, we cannot perform at our best unless we also take care of our physical needs.

In a quest to increase public consciousness of how wellbeing can be supported, those working on the Foresight project asked the New Economics Foundation to research and identify the wellbeing equivalent of five fruit and vegetables a day. They identified the following:

- Connect
- Be Active
- Take Notice
- Keep Learning
- Give

---

21   Kolappa, K., Henderson, D. C. & Kishore, S. P. (1 January 2013): No physical health without mental health. *Bulletin of the World Health Organisation*, 3-3A.

22   Shah, S. A. (2012): *Well-being patterns uncovered*. London: New Economics Foundation.

The authors of the report judged those five as the most likely to be accessible to everyone. They are defined sufficiently broadly to allow for multiple interpretations that still achieve the desired result. In the same way as the model of five pieces of fruit or vegetables every day, they allow much choice within a broad framework and thus avoid the strictures that often deter us from following such advice. I managed to achieve all of these in a single day when I travelled to Exeter by train for a course (keep learning). I walked to the railway station (be active); met new people on the course (connect); gave directions to a stranger to find the road he was looking for (give/connect), and paused on the walk home to notice a beautiful magnolia tree in full bloom in the local churchyard (take notice). Still, there was something missing: what the original data set omitted was one frequently ignored fundamental human need: sleep.

The importance of sleep

Just as wellbeing underpins emotional resilience, so we need to recognise that sleep underpins wellbeing. From amoeba to man, every living creature has some sort of sleep/wake cycle. Advances in neuroscience are beginning to unravel some of the mysteries of sleep and its attendant circadian rhythm. Sleep seems likely to have a restorative function, a bit like the update process on your computer, and there is much evidence of its impact on our ability to sustain memory, and thus to learn new skills.

Experiments show that we are more able to make reasoned decisions, we are more creative and better at problem-solving when we are rested. The sleep-deprived brain behaves similarly to a brain under the influence of alcohol: people take more risks when they are sleep-deprived and they are less able to take in information through the five senses. Motorway signs reminding us that 'tiredness kills' and that we should 'take a break' are indicative of increased knowledge of the impact of sleep deprivation on our ability to concentrate and react promptly to external stimuli. We know that a good night's sleep gives us a better chance of 'feeling good' and 'functioning well'. Many of us will have had the experience of grappling with a problem at night, which miraculously seems to be easily solved in the morning. A lack of sleep has a negative impact on our mood, so we are less able to 'feel good'. Awaking well rested and ready for the day ahead gives us the best chance of making decisions during the day that will support our long-term goals.

New York used to be known as the city that never sleeps. Today, that label belongs to our 'always on' society and a working climate where everything is moving faster. We used to be content to send letters to each other and wait several days for a response. Email has largely put an end to that approach. Email is easy; it has taught us not to wait. With the mobile phone's capacity for retrieving email, and the tendency to have our mobile phones about our person, we need never be disconnected from work.

Those who use their mobile phone as an alarm clock frequently confess to checking their emails in the middle of the night. In fact, scientists in Holland have identified another phenomenon related to insufficient sleep: bedtime procrastination, which they define as 'going to bed later than intended, without having external reasons for doing so'[23]. Completing 'just one more task' before bedtime can hijack our intention to establish a proper sleep routine. Conversations with coaching clients prove that I am not the only person who sets an alarm on my computer to tell me when it is time to close down, ignore it, lose track of time, and spend another half an hour working, even though the voice in my head is screaming 'for goodness sake, go to bed!'

---

23   Kroese, F. M. (2016): Bedtime procrastination. *Journal of Health Psychology*, 21 (5), pp. 853-862.

According to Professor Russell Foster[24], as a nation we sleep on average one to two hours less than we did in 1950, and most of us do not recognise when we are sleep deprived. 31% of drivers in a US study reported falling asleep at the wheel without warning. A BBC television documentary[25] explained to its viewers how to carry out a 'sleep onset latency test'.

Exercise 3: The sleep onset latency test

Lie down on a bed during the afternoon holding a metal spoon above a metal tray that is placed on the floor adjacent to your bed. When you lie down, note the time, or start a timer. Close your eyes.

When you fall asleep, the spoon will fall from your grasp, clatter on to the metal tray, and wake you up.

If 15 minutes pass and you are still awake, you are not sleep deprived.

If you fall asleep within ten minutes you are moderately sleep deprived

If it takes less than five minutes for you to fall asleep, you are severely sleep deprived. Consider adopting some of the habits identified below.

With advances in MRI scanning and neuroscience, scientists have never been in a better position to assess the impact of sleeplessness on the functioning of the brain. It appears that nearly half the US and UK population is not getting enough sleep[26]. Do not imagine that because sleep deprivation is common, it is unimportant. Tiredness really does kill. There are reasons beyond our control that might deny us sleep, or interfere with our light/dark circadian rhythm. For parents of young children, for those whose professions require that they are on call during the night, and for many shift workers, feeling well rested is a phenomenon they can only dimly recall. Shift workers are more vulnerable to a number of health risks (including cardiovascular disease, type-2 diabetes, obesity and stroke) due to constantly denying the body the light/dark cycle it needs to follow.

---

24   Foster, R. (17 March 2017): *BBC iplayer radio.* Available at: www.bbc.co.uk/programmes/ b08hz9yw [Accessed: 22 March 2017].

25   BBC Television. (1 June 2017): *The Truth about Sleep.* (1 June 2017). Available at: www.bbc. co.uk/programmes/p05lyc7s [Accessed: 18 July 2017].

26   Culpin, V. (2018): *The Business of Sleep.* London: Bloomsbury.

Getting a good night's sleep

During the day

- Reduce caffeine: it increases cortisol.
- Make time for physical exercise: it lowers levels of cortisol.
- Keep the bedroom work-free: it needs to be a space that your body associates with sleep.
- Avoid heavy meals late in the evening and try to eat at least an hour before bedtime: a heavy meal makes demands on your digestive system, just when it is shutting down.

Towards the evening

- Avoid caffeinated drinks after noon: caffeine stays in the system for between five to nine hours after consumption.
- Avoid relying on alcohol as a sedative: it may send you to sleep, but it upsets the functioning of your natural circadian rhythm and is likely to lead you to wake during the night.
- Avoid using bright light, particularly that which emanates from an electronic screen, for at least an hour before bedtime: bright light tells our system to wake up.
- Set a time to switch off from work; if necessary, set an alarm to remind you – or get someone else to nag you.
- Gradually lower light levels; if you read in bed use a light with a low wattage.
- Establish a bedtime routine and follow it: routine helps to signal to your body that it is time to sleep.

At night

- Ensure the bedroom is really dark and cool: your core body temperature needs to drop to induce sleep.
- If you have an alarm clock with an LED display, cover the display.
- If you wake up during the night avoid checking the clock: such activity demands that you are more alert.

- Rid your room of distractions, including your mobile phone. Invest in an old- fashioned alarm clock rather than using your mobile phone.
- If you habitually visit the bathroom during the night, avoid turning on the light: bright light signals to your system it is time to be alert.
- Keep a notebook by the bed to jot down those 2am thoughts so you're not trying to hold on to them.
- Accept that you will sometimes find it difficult to get back to sleep: focus on your breathing, counting your breaths, listen to the radio quietly, or (yes, really) count sheep. Monotony helps.
- Keep a sleep diary like the one below: forensically analyse the data to identify what supports or undermines your ability to gain a good night's sleep.

Exercise 4: Sleep diary

This is to complete last thing at night before you go to bed.

Days of the week							
How many caffeinated drinks did you have before 5pm?							
How many caffeinated drinks did you have after 5pm?							
How many alcohol units before 5pm?..							
... and how many after 5pm?							
In minutes, how much exercise did you take today before 9pm?							
... and similarly, after 9pm?							
What medication have you taken today, if any?							

Days of the week								
How much sleep did you take in minutes during the day (if any)?								
Have you felt any of the following today: Tired? Impatient? Unable to concentrate? Irritable? Unusually emotional?								
In the hour before bedtime what did your routine include?								

Sleep diary Complete on waking first thing in the morning

Day of the week								
What time did you go to bed last night?								
What time did you wake this morning?								
How many minutes did it take you to fall asleep?								
Did you fall asleep a) Easily? b) After a little time? c) With difficulty?								
How many times did you wake in the night?								
How long were you awake in the night in total?								
What disturbed your sleep (eg, noise, cold, worry, discomfort)?								
How would you rate the quality of sleep from 1-5 (poor to very good)?								

Day of the week								
How do you feel this morning? a) Refreshed b) Okay c) Lethargic								
Any other observations?								

Bleary eyed, I reach to turn off the radio alarm, set sufficiently early to allow me to get up in time to go to the gym before I start work. 'I knew I should have turned off my computer before the last episode of that series started,' I think to myself. I lie there, deep in conversation with myself. 'Could I have another 20 minutes and go to the gym this evening instead?' 'No, you are out this evening' 'Perhaps I could go tomorrow morning instead? Is it so bad to miss a day?' 'Remember you have to be out early tomorrow morning'. 'But I really don't have any energy' So the dialogue continues, illustrating that it is easier to pay attention to our immediate needs (to finish watching the TV series) rather than paying attention to the long-term impact of sleep deprivation.

Paying attention to our wellbeing requires conscious effort. I highlight sleep as being the first step in supporting wellbeing, because we are more able to take control after a good night's sleep. Until actions that support wellbeing become habitual, they require willpower, or what scientists refer to as 'self-regulation'. Experiments suggest that self-regulatory strength is finite; like a muscle, it can be strengthened and it can be overused[27]. Unlike a muscle, which aches to tell us we have done too much, we are unaware of its overuse. We can observe only the consequences of low self-regulatory strength, for example when we stay up later than intended, or have an additional glass of wine when we know it will make it harder to get out of bed in the morning. Experiments have shown that self-regulation improves after a period of rest and we know instinctively that we feel more in control when we are well rested. When we take sleep seriously, we are at the start of building a virtuous circle that can have a positive impact on our performance and our ability to take the right decisions, manage our emotions, interact productively with others and generally carry out the infinite range of executive functions required of leaders.

If you have no routine to help you to wind down, you may well still be alert when you go to bed. Sleep comes later than intended and in the morning several cups of coffee help you to feel ready for the day. Remember that caffeine remains in the system between five and nine hours. If you are consuming caffeine in the afternoon, you are likely to be alert when your body needs sleep, so a glass of wine or equivalent will help you to relax. While it will help you to sleep, it acts as sedative, so it sedates the whole system, including the parts which are used in restoration. When the sedative wears off, you are likely to experience interrupted sleep and awake feeling tired, to reach for the caffeine again, and so it goes on.

---

27   Segerstrom, S. & Ness, S. L. (2007): Heart Rate Variability Reflects Self-Regulatory Strength, Effort and Fatigue. *Psychological Science*, 18 (3), pp. 275-281.

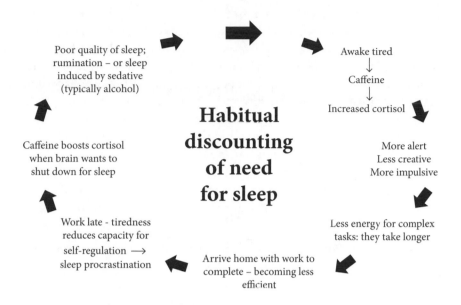

Figure 2: The sleep-deprivation cycle

When my children were little, and worrying about what might happen the next day at school, we always reminded them 'all shadows look longer by candlelight'. It is a phrase they still remember today. Obstacles that seem overwhelming when considered at the end of a long day often diminish in size when daytime comes. According to neuroscientist Penelope Lewis: 'sleep deprived people are more easily frustrated, intolerant, unforgiving, uncaring and self-absorbed than they would be if they were properly rested.'[28]If it appears self-indulgent to allow yourself more sleep, just think of those you live with and do it for their sake.

If you are a car driver, one of the things you are likely to do is to top up fuel levels before the tank is empty. You are also likely to ensure that your car is serviced regularly to keep it in good running order. When it comes to taking care of our bodies, most of us simply expect them to keep going regardless of how we treat them. We know about the effects of poor diet, inadequate sleep, minimal exercise, too much caffeine or alcohol, and yet we continue to ignore the potential impact on ourselves.

---

28   Lewis, P. A. (2013): *The Secret World of Sleep*. New York: Palgrave Macmillan.

During a research interview, I raised the subject of wellbeing with my interviewee. 'Oh yes,' she said, 'I did a questionnaire about that the other day. It didn't tell me anything I didn't know already – that I should take more exercise, sleep more and drink less alcohol'. We know these things but find it hard to act on them. Newspaper reports concerning people who have done all the 'wrong' things to stay healthy and yet have lived into their 90s give us hope. Margaret Heffernan has written about the human inclination towards 'wilful blindness'. As human beings (and thus as leaders) we are inclined to discount anything that challenges our world view and – more than that – we look for evidence that supports our prejudices. If you see yourself as a strong leader, you will probably find it hard to acknowledge that you could also be sufficiently vulnerable to succumb to the effects of prolonged stress, which impacts on both mind and body.

Professor Russell Foster, Director of the Sleep and Circadian Neuroscience Institute at the University of Oxford, sees sleep as quite simply 'the most effective cognitive enhancer we've got.'[29] If that is true, and it does indeed underpin wellbeing, organisations whose *raison d'etre* is learning cannot afford to ignore it.

Wellbeing in education

The workforce of publicly funded UK schools and other public sector organisations is under pressure to achieve more than ever with budgets, which are reducing in real terms and significantly reduced support services. Time in the working day is finite; if you spend time with your family when you get home, the likelihood is that you will be working late into the night. Those who work in offices or spend a fair proportion of their working day engaged in electronic communication can easily overlook the challenges faced by those whose roles force them to use evenings and weekends to deal with an ever-increasing flood of email. The tyranny of email can contribute significantly to individuals' difficulty in turning off at the end of the day, or when they get home in the evening. Leaders can help create a wellbeing culture by ensuring there is clarity over electronic communication: how important is it? What is it used for? What are the organisation's demands (and taboos)

---

29   Foster, R. (17 March 2017): *BBC iplayer radio*. Available at: http://www.bbc.co.uk/ programmes/b08hz9yw [Accessed: 22 March 2017].

with regard to the need to reply? Whatever you say as a school leader about your commitment to wellbeing, if you are staying at school later than everyone else and sending and responding to emails late into the evening, the message is clear: this is the way we work in this school.

Exhaustion can become a status symbol, particularly if you are demanding a great deal from staff that are feeling overburdened. Many of the leaders I work with tell me they feel guilty if they come in late the day after they have been at school until 10pm (or later) at a governors' meeting the night before. They strive to normalise their experience: 'No one has a lunch break'; 'no one leaves school before 6pm,' they protest, justifying their own practice. My answer is always the same: just because it is normal, that does not mean it is healthy. In the early days of Ofsted inspections I joined a team inspecting a special school that was managing the challenging behaviour of students exceptionally well – a rarity in those days.

'You must be drained,' commented one of the team to the head one day. 'No,' he replied, 'I'm not drained. My staff may be: they work incredibly hard. If they get into difficulties and I am equally drained, who is going to help them out?' However tired the crew, someone needs to be able to steer the ship if it is not to end up on the rocks where all will perish. It is in times of crisis that leaders really earn their pay. They have a responsibility to guard against exhaustion so that they always have personal resources available when things become really difficult. 'It is not about being self-indulgent or selfish, it is about having a proper and appropriate regard for personal growth and sustainability.'[30]

Before working in education, I worked in a large publishing company, reporting to a director who was frequently faced with the task of turning down publishing proposals. Feelings of rejection led to some difficult encounters with authors, but my boss had his eye on the big picture and would not be deterred: 'my first duty to my authors,' he said to me early on, 'is to keep the company in business.' I have often shared a variation of this with headteachers. 'Your first duty to the school is to keep yourself *in business.*' By which I mean able to function at your best and keep something in reserve.

---

30   West-Burnham, J. (2009): *Rethinking Educational Leadership.* London: Continuum International Publishing Group.

Taking sick leave during term time may feel like letting the side down, but struggling on often causes greater difficulties in the long-term. A young headteacher who decided to ignore continuing pain following a suspected heart attack, rather than visiting a doctor; the headteacher who did not realise she was running on empty until she found she couldn't cope in school and spent increasing amounts of time away, focusing on outside priorities; the headteacher who suffered an anxiety attack when he was due to address a parents' meeting. To these, illness was an indication of weakness and weakness and leadership make unhappy companions.

We may have said goodbye in schools to the 'hero head' model, but it seems that vestiges of the importance of invincibility for a strong leader remain. Surviving physical attack was important for leaders of troops in battles past. The strength that is required in 21st century society calls for a different type of invincibility. However, it leaves leaders and followers with a dilemma: followers want their leaders to be approachable and human; they do not want them to be vulnerable – yet to be human is to be vulnerable.

Teachers and school leaders are strongly aware of the need to support the mental health and wellbeing of their students. In 2016 the Mental Health Taskforce produced their recommendations for a five year plan to address mental ill-health[31]. Statistics quoted focusing on the history of those with chronic mental ill-health, reveal the importance of early intervention. 50% of adults suffering with chronic mental ill-health had symptoms before the age of 14; 75% of sufferers showed symptoms before the age of 24. The charity *Young Minds* estimates that three children in every class in the country has a diagnosable mental health disorder: 850,000 children across the UK.

Schools often seem to be regarded by government as the 'universal fixing agent': from the requirement for provision of before- and after-school care, to the teaching of British values and the implementation of the 'prevent' anti-terrorist strategy. When there is deemed to be a malaise

---

31   Mental Health Taskforce. (2016): *The Five Year Forward View for Mental Health*. London: NHS England. Available at: www.england.nhs.uk/wp-content/uploads/2016/02/Mental-Health-Taskforce-FYFV-final.pdf

in society, schools are required to address it. As successive governments pass their anxiety concerning the prosperity of their citizens down the line, it is felt in schools as an additional pressure. Leaders find themselves putting new demands on staff to squeeze more into the school day; teachers make additional demands on students. Stress undermines individuals' ability to perform at their best. Now the mental health of their students has been added to schools' priorities. It is like a grim game of pass the parcel. When leaders fail to adjust quickly enough to new requirements – when they take too long to unwrap their layer of the parcel before passing it on – the music stops and, all too often, they are taken out of the game.

School leaders, then, are faced with a constant juggling act. They know the school will be judged largely on academic results; they know that too much pressure to achieve impacts negatively on emotional wellbeing and mental health of students and staff. They are called to 'square the circle of meeting the demands of increasingly intensive work, whilst preserving and nurturing wellbeing.'[32]

---

32   Government Office for Science. (2008): *Mental Capital and Wellbeing Summary*. London: HMSO.

Their choices seem limited to:

- Absorb the stress and suffer the consequences.
- Pass the stress down the line to teachers, who in turn may pass it on to students or absorb it themselves (or, indeed, both).
- Accept that their quest to support the wellbeing of others may be judged as a distraction from aiming for high academic results and risk the consequences.
- Recognise the danger of absorbing the stress and find means of letting it go.
- Leave the profession, or at least give up the role that makes them ultimately accountable.

How you manage this juggling act as a leader will depend on a number of factors, including your own confidence in your leadership, the context in which you are working, and support from the governors and the community. What matters in maintaining your wellbeing, is that you are aware of the interplay of the system and its impact on you and the community. We all know the aeroplane safety instructions that highlight the importance of putting the oxygen mask on ourselves before trying to help others. There is a difference between having knowledge and acting on it. It is too easy to think the advice is for others and not relevant to us.

In chapter one, I refer to the survey of headteachers I carried out as part of my MEd research, which revealed that those who had been longest in headship were more inclined to worry that they were not good enough. I analysed all the results with reference to time in headship. Participants were asked to agree or disagree with a number of statements, including: 'I take care to look after my own health and wellbeing.' The graph below represents their response.

It is worth noting that those who had been longest in headship, who were more inclined to worry that they were not good enough, were also those who paid least attention to their own health and wellbeing. Once you accept the need to look after your own health and wellbeing as a leader, you are more likely to be able to develop the habits outlined by the New Economics Foundation's five-a-day recommendation. There is evidence of teachers who engage with social media beginning to prioritise their wellbeing, thanks to the #teacher5aday movement on Twitter and the general advice given by NEF. Here are some additional thoughts on how to build your five-a-day habit.

I take care to look after my health and wellbeing

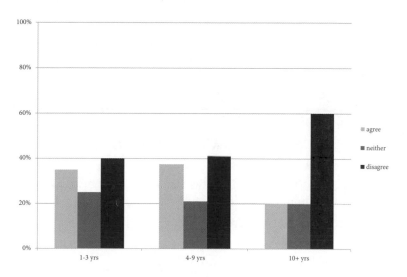

Time in headship

Figure 3: Attention to wellbeing by time in headship

Connect

'I wish I had stayed in touch with my friends' – failure to connect is one of the top five regrets of the dying identified by Bronnie Ware[33]. She captured the top five regrets from patients' stories during her time working as a live-in carer to a succession of terminally ill patients. The support of family and friends was identified in my research as the number-one activity that supports resilience. Most will acknowledge that relationships with family and friends require nurturing if they are

---

33   Ware, B. (2011): *The Top Five Regrets of the Dying*. London: Hay House.

to flourish. It is not always easy to prioritise those relationships and invest time in them. After a day spent at work managing relationships with work colleagues, acting 'professionally', choosing words carefully in order to ensure they lead to the outcome we are looking for, it is no wonder that we have little energy left when we get home. We take off our professional persona, because at home we are loved and accepted. We are not on our guard, ensuring that we say the right thing. At work we may go out of our way to give feedback to colleagues and ensure they know they are valued.

It is easy to assume that those at home already know we value them, so there is no need to tell them with words (or more importantly) in action. Noticing how you connect with others is a crucial step towards ensuring that your life does not become overwhelmed by the job.

Check your connections

- Check out how – and how often – you are connecting with family and friends.
- Make a point of taking time to be with members of your family without distraction.
- Be present when you are with them.
- Notice if you feel resentful of 'having' to engage with family or friends when you have work to do.
- Remind yourself every day that – however important your job – you are infinitely more replaceable in your job than at home.

Be active

If you are a natural runner, play golf or another active sport every weekend, cycle to work daily, or otherwise ensure that you take regular exercise, now is the moment to congratulate yourself, feel pleased that you have established this helpful habit and pass on to the next section. If this is a struggle for you, however, you will need to invest some time and effort on something that you are probably already telling yourself you will never maintain.

Advice from health professionals regarding what constitutes sufficient exercise to have a positive impact on our health appears to change regularly. The current guidance is to take at least 150 minutes of moderate aerobic exercise a week (that is brisk walking or cycling) or 75 minutes of vigorous exercise a week, plus some muscle strengthening exercise. The advice included in the NEF protocol is more pragmatic: 'Discover a physical activity you enjoy and that suits your level of mobility and fitness.'

Health professionals are clear that if you gain very little exercise, any increase in activity is going to be an improvement. Many headteachers I have spoken to say they would find it difficult to walk round the playing field, for example … what would everybody think? A health and safety check is always a good explanation. If you are head of a school with a reasonably large site, simply walking round building will provide some exercise, and there is always the 'excuse', if you need one, of monitoring. 'But people see me as available and constantly stop me to ask questions,' wailed one school leader I spoke to. 'Just carry a file and look purposeful,' responded another. 'Then you'll look as though you're on a mission and if anyone tries to stop you then you can indicate it's vital that you deliver this file to the intended recipient without delay.'

There are many electronic devices that will monitor the number of steps you take a day (10,000 being what most people aim for). If you find yourself sitting for most of the day, setting an alarm to ensure you get up and walk (ideally outside) even briefly every hour will help guard against inertia.

Perhaps there is an activity you used to enjoy which you have not done for a long time. Consider taking it up again. Exercise does not have to be sport. A friend of mine recently took up salsa dancing, something she had not done since university, and now takes her exercise that way. I sometimes conduct coaching sessions while walking. There is something about movement that can unlock the key to the challenge that may have been going round and round in my client's head. Taking a walk to think through a difficulty, alone or with your coach, can be beneficial for your emotional, physical and cognitive wellbeing.

Finally, consider how 'nudging' might help to develop more helpful habits. Nudging is a concept from behavioural economics that involves changing what is called the 'choice architecture' that influences our decisions. The argument is that people do not always act rationally, but they do tend to behave in predictable ways. You might need to do some forensic analysis of your own habits in order to find the change that will influence you to do something different. For me, it was finding radio serials to listen to on my phone while exercising in my local gym. Wanting to know what happens next was sufficient incentive to get me to the gym; once there, it wasn't so hard to exercise. In Stockholm, a study revealed that when faced with the choice between climbing stairs or riding on the escalator, people chose to take the stairs 66% more often when the stairs looked and sounded like a piano. A friend supported her husband's drive to get fit by putting his running shoes where he would practically trip over them first thing in the morning. A colleague regretting that he had taken up smoking again because it was too easy to stop at the shop on the way home and pick up a packet of cigarettes, started parking in a different place in his work car park, so that it was logical to drive home by a different route and not pass the shop.

Activity for the habitually inactive

- Don't set yourself up to fail by expecting the impossible. Remember any increase in activity will help.
- Use a fitness tracker (you can buy one or download for free onto your phone).
- Don't rule out walking and talking if someone wants to discuss something with you.
- Revisit old pastimes that kept you active.
- Change your 'choice architecture'.

I'm scheduled to spend the day at a course on stress management. I don't really suffer from stress, I tell myself, but it will be useful to know how to support the staff who work with me. As I am getting ready, I receive a call from a colleague who is due to run some computer training on a particular online platform that day. The site is unexpectedly down for maintenance and he wants to be able to contact those who are due to be trained, in order to tell them not to come. It is 7:30am – too soon for the administrator to be in the office. I make some suggestions, send a couple of emails, and hope that luck is on our side and that everyone who was due to attend will receive the necessary information before setting out. Now it is 7:45am; I need to leave in the next 15 minutes to reach my destination in time to join the registration process, and I haven't finished dressing, let alone had breakfast. 8:10am sees me hurtling through the Somerset lanes. 'I can't be late for a session on stress management,' I tell myself. My guardian angel is working overtime: I reach my destination in record time, find a parking place almost immediately, and I am just in time to join the end of the line of delegates walking from the coffee station to the training room. In the first session we talk in pairs and I am struck by how little autonomy my partner has in his job. 'How stressful that must be,' I tell myself, 'no wonder he feels stressed'. It is only when we walk back to the coffee station at 10:30am that I notice that I am wearing shoes that don't match: one is blue and the other black. But of course, I don't do stress.

Take notice

Ten years after this stress management course, I decided to sign up for the mindfulness-based stress-reduction (MBSR) eight-week course. As I was still unable to acknowledge that I might be someone who suffers from stress, I told myself that I was signing up to the course so that I could discover whether it might be useful to my clients.

On the MBSR course I learned that our minds inevitably wander off on their own, and that practising mindfulness is a way of keeping them focused on the present moment. Jon Kabat-Zinn, a leading practitioner of mindfulness, defines mindfulness as paying attention in a particular way, on purpose, in the present moment, non-judgementally. An added potential benefit for me was the thought that the accent on focus 'in the moment' might improve my confidence as a church organist. I feel reasonably competent – as long as no one is listening. If I could focus on the music rather than the mistakes I might make, or had just made when playing in public, it might make playing more enjoyable for the congregation and myself.

At about the same time that I was thinking about signing up for the course, I had recently visited the doctor (an activity which always challenges my self-image as a fit and healthy person). I had woken one morning to find that my head was locked in one position and moving it caused considerable pain. It was several weeks later, following visits to the doctor, conversations with my coach, and a consultation with an Alexander technique specialist, that I had to acknowledge that the difficulty was caused by a stressful situation I was dealing with in my private life. As I practised mindfulness daily for the duration of the eight-week course, I noticed that my mind and body seem to spend their time disconnected from each other during the course of a normal day. It is a hazard of modern life: we rush from one event to the next with no time to pause and notice how we are feeling physically. And yet, if only we could notice how we are feeling, we might be able to take remedial action before pain becomes acute and demands our attention.

Noticing how our bodies are feeling is only one aspect of 'take notice', however. On the MBSR course we were taught to pause over positive images or events for 20 seconds in order to ensure that they would remain in our minds. Many of the leaders I coach can give me a list of things that have gone badly during the preceding week and struggle to be able to name things that have gone well. This is not because nothing ever goes right for them, but because we are programmed to remember the events or circumstances that cause us difficulties. Those that do run smoothly we tend to gloss over and take for granted. Despite all the technological advances of recent years, and the changes in society, our brains have remained largely unchanged for over a hundred thousand years.

If our ancestors were to survive, it was important for them to remember events that threatened them. We are no different. We remember events that lead us into difficulty; they, not the happy memories, are the ones that keep us awake at night. 'Good memories act like Teflon; bad memories act like Velcro' is a mantra which remained with me from the course. When I was a child I learned the poem *Leisure* by William Henry Davis which starts: 'what is life if, full of care, we have no time to stand and stare?' Only now, many years later, have I realised how important it is to 'stand and stare'.

I can verify the usefulness of the 20-second rule. Fed up of spending precious moments in the day looking for something I had put down somewhere (reading glasses, car keys, purse) I now try to pause long enough to make a mental note. I 'stand and stare' at the object for seconds and even occasionally say aloud 'I am putting my [object] here'. It is not a perfect system, but I now spend far less time looking for things that I have put down without noticing where.

When I started the MBSR course, I was expected to practise mindfulness for 30 minutes at least five times a week. I thought that one day it would be easy and I would become sufficiently expert that I no longer needed to practise. As we drew to the end of the eight-week course, I realised that 'my practice' meant what I do habitually every day, just as we talk about a doctor's 'practice'. In the same way as maintaining a healthy weight means maintaining healthy eating habits, rather than yo-yo dieting, mindfulness – taking notice in the present moment – is a way of life.

You could start by taking notice of what gives you a greater sense of wellbeing. It does not have to mean adding something to your already crowded schedule. It could be something as simple as changing the music you listen to, finding a different route to and from work, or even changing the picture on your computer desktop. I recently changed a beautiful grey and slightly menacing view in the Lake District for the bright yellows, blues and greens of the Somerset levels in the spring sunshine. I felt my mood lift immediately.

Take notice and be present

- Value process. Cleaning your teeth, washing up, ironing. Make an effort to notice the experience, rather than mentally being somewhere else.
- Sign up for a mindfulness course, or find your own way. You can Google search 'mindfulness meditation' for many leads and free meditation practices.
- Set an app on your phone/put a reminder in your office to **S**TOP; **T**ake a breath; **O**bserve how you're feeling, physically, mentally and emotionally; **P**roceed mindfully.
- Pay attention to what your body is telling you. Backache? Headaches? Indigestion? Nausea? Any of these could be signs of stress and could develop into something more serious if ignored.
- At the end of a day/week (whatever works for you) write down things that have gone well so that you have them to refer to when things get tough.
- Notice your environment: stop and stare; bring the outside in with flowers or plants. Remove barriers to productive working: the drawer that sticks; the photocopier that jams; the squeaky castor that irritates.
- Identify small changes in routine (Radio 3, not Radio 4; walk, not drive; saying 'maybe' instead of 'yes') that contribute to your sense of wellbeing.

We spend so much time functioning on auto-pilot, not questioning the habits that have developed over time; it can be beneficial bring those habits in to consciousness once in a while and decide whether the same tasks could be accomplished in a way that contributes to our wellbeing.

Keep learning

The NEF guidance specifically suggests proactively finding something new to learn. 'Try something new. Rediscover an old interest. Sign up for that course.' For professional facilitators of learning, putting ourselves in a formal learning position has the added advantage of increasing our empathy for the learners we engage with. It forces us to do what we expect of others: it makes us vulnerable. Of course, as human beings, we are vulnerable but many of us strive to keep this truth out of our consciousness.

The research that underpins the NEF five-a-day makes clear that learning in an environment that involves setting a goal and achieving that goal is in part what accounts for the contribution made to wellbeing; so the sense of achievement may be, at least, as rewarding as the learning itself. It is important to set realistic goals. A small change can have a significant impact, but when you are beginning to develop a new habit, be careful to avoid setting yourself up to fail. Early in my coaching career I coached someone who felt he needed to behave differently in a number of ways, including starting to exercise. His solution was to set himself a goal of getting up (to my mind, impossibly) early every morning and going for a run. I was negligent in not asking him to do a reality check and suggesting that he start with something rather less demanding. Only in talking it through with my supervisor did I realise how great the challenge my client had set himself. Not surprisingly, he did not achieve his ambition and what he regarded as a failure did nothing to improve his self-esteem and ability to take control, nor his wellbeing.

At its most basic, I think of 'keep learning', as being open-minded and curious about life. When we close down our capacity for critical thinking, or assume that we have life sorted, we risk giving up on life. Education should surely lead the field amongst the professions that require professional learning as part of their accreditation process. Imagine visiting a doctor who had not kept abreast of new developments, or a solicitor or accountant who had not noticed the introduction of new laws that affect the advice they give. As a chair of governors, I recall my frustration when a fellow-governor told me that she had not known how to do something. 'What stopped you from asking?' I enquired. 'I'm one of those people who has to be in the right mood to ask for help,' came the reply. Thank goodness she was not a surgeon who needed advice about a patient she was about to operate on. If schools are places of learning, leaders (including governors) should have 'keep learning' as a mantra.

Leaders need to be especially open to learning about themselves in order to be able to interact more effectively with others. The challenge for leaders in all contexts is to promote a climate where mistakes are seen as opportunities for learning, despite the risks of being judged as 'failing' if we get it wrong.

Keep learning

The more you know, the more you know you don't know.

- Be curious; look for explanations.
- Take time to satisfy your curiosity with the help of Google or another search engine.
- Put yourself in the situation of a learner.
- If you leave a course thinking 'I haven't learned anything new' ask yourself: 'what have I learned about myself and what am I going to do about it?'
- Share your learning goals with others.
- Be prepared to be vulnerable.

Give

Researchers at the University of British Columbia and Harvard Business School collaborated on a study to discover whether the way individuals spend their money is at least as influential on their happiness as the amount of income they receive. They found that spending more of one's income on others predicted greater happiness for the donor. The University of Notre Dame was the home of the 'Science of Generosity Initiative' involving a wide-ranging study of the beliefs and practices regarding generosity of hundreds of Americans. *The Paradox of Giving*[34] concludes that giving to others does not have to involve money to be beneficial to the donor. Giving time, encouragement, emotional availability, attention, all benefit the donor. A review of studies[35] reveals

---

34 Smith, C. & Davidson, H. (2014): *The Paradox of Generosity.* New York: Oxford Universtiy Press.
35 Cooper, C. L. & Hupert, F. A. (2014): *Wellbeing: A Complete Reference Guide, Volume 6.* Chichester: John Wiley & Sons Ltd.

clear physical and psychological benefits that emanate from giving time and money to others. A variety of explanations are proposed, including the sense of satisfaction achieved by making a difference to the lives of others, and the triggering of the release of oxytocin in the brain – the hormone implicated in mother-infant bonding.

As I alight from the London train a young woman asks me whether I know the location of a particular building in the town. She speaks in broken English, but I understand that she is due there for an interview. I am not sure whether she understands my directions, so I decide to take a longer walk home so that I can accompany her to within sight of her destination, to be sure that she does not miss her interview. We do our best to converse as we walk; it is hard going, but she is clearly very grateful to me for walking with her.

Such small gestures support our wellbeing, partly because they allow us to connect with others, but also because the very act of giving can give us a sense of wellbeing.

The drive to make a difference to the lives of others is what attracts many of its practitioners into the public sector. There is some evidence that public sector workers find their lives more satisfying that those in the private sector.[36] Many of us in the 'helping' professions (coaching, counselling, therapy, nursing, social care and so on) will verify that we gain at least as much from giving to our clients or patients as they gain.

Society relies increasingly on willing volunteers to serve the needs of others. They may be family members or those working for charities, helping at the local foodbank, the church fete, or at their local school. Most of us need to feel needed. We would be wise to be conscious of our boundaries when we offer help to others, however, if we are not to end up feeling taken for granted or resentful. Many people would rather not volunteer in the first place than risk being unable to exit from a role they have volunteered to undertake. If you are offering to help one day a week, for example, be clear whether one day is easier than another, make sure to define what 'a day' means – is it five, six, or seven hours?

---

36   Shah, S. A. (2012): *Well-being patterns uncovered*. London: New Economics Foundation.

And, for how many weeks or months are you volunteering? It is always a good idea to agree in advance a time when both parties can review the arrangement and agree whether it is working equally well for them both. Far better a few moments of discomfort as you discuss the pros and cons of an arrangement, than months of mounting resentment that weigh you down, undermine your wellbeing and cancel out the positive feelings that emanate from giving willingly.

Give

- Give what you can, when you can, because you want to, rather than because you feel you should.
- Take time to consider how you feel about giving: from giving money to charities or rough sleepers on the streets, to giving time to support others. Having thought about it in advance, you are more likely to respond than react when faced with a request.
- If you see someone without a smile, give them one of yours.

You may already have completed the exercise in chapter 1, to help you focus on what supports and what undermines your emotional resilience. If you look at that alongside the five-a-day outlined by the New Economics Foundation report, you may find some common issues, so that you can focus on both your emotional resilience and your wellbeing at the same time. I hope it is becoming clear that the model presented at the beginning of this book is simply an aid to structuring how we think about supporting emotional resilience. There are no clear boundaries between the various contributing factors. Being able to operate as – and gradually become – an integrated human being is a journey that demands self-compassion, and yet we often give compassion to others far more easily than to ourselves.

Imagine the person you love more than anyone in the world. Imagine they are in solitary confinement and you are forced to act as their jailer, constantly depriving them of sleep, and driving them to work harder when they protest they are tired. Imagine administering drugs to them so that they can meet your demands, and ignoring their protests that they have had enough. Imagine giving them food only when you remember, and forgetting to let them out of their cell for fresh air and exercise.

Get the picture? If you would not treat someone you love in this way, why is it okay to do it to yourself?

Worth remembering

- You owe it to yourself and to the organisation you lead, to take care of your own health and wellbeing. Just as your car needs regular servicing to keep going without breaking down, so do you.
- You need to get the right amount of sleep to function at your best.
- Being well rested helps you to see things in proportion: all shadows look longer by candlelight.
- Self-regulation is like a muscle; it strengthens the more you use it, and works less effectively when you are tired.

Looking after your health and wellbeing gives you the best chance of maintaining the energy you need to carry out your day-to-day responsibilities and have energy left over to engage in leisure activities. Let us consider now what else might drain or energise us, and how we use the energy we have.

Chapter Three: Energy

In the Albert Hall the silence is tangible: it is the silence of 6,000 people holding their breath, captured in a moment of timeless eternity. The conductor's arms are held aloft, caught in freeze frame, as he pays silent and respectful homage to the creation of the transitory work of art of which he is a part. On the stage the musicians wait to be released from the spell they have conjured. The conductor's shoulders soften and, as he gently lowers his arms, the hall erupts in a wave of appreciative applause. He takes out his handkerchief and mops his brow.

It is quite clear that the leader of this 'organisation' has expended all his energy in this performance, and yet to the uninitiated he appears to have done very little other than wave his arms around. We know perfectly well that the orchestra could continue without him. Indeed, some conductors have even demonstrated this by leaving the podium during a performance. It would be impossible for him to have realised his vision alone. He is not even capable of playing each of the orchestral parts on his own. He must rely on his team for the technical expertise required to play each of the instruments. Even if he trained as a violinist, an organist, or bassoonist, he will have lost some of his technical skills while concentrating on his conducting. His role is one of leadership: he creates the vision, communicates the vision so that each instrumentalist can understand in terms of his or her own context, and throughout the performance he prompts, adjusts, inspires and energises his team with just the right amount of encouragement. He must be so confident of his own expertise that he no longer needs to focus on himself: his mission is to use his energy to effect change through others.

If you are required to achieve results through others, some of the aspects of your role that consume energy will be clearly visible and obvious; some are not. If you have ever sunk down at the end of a day and said to yourself 'why am I so tired?' you are probably unaware of where some of your energy goes. If you want to be as smart in managing your energy account as you are in managing your budget, you need to check where your energy goes, and if necessary, manage it differently. We considered in the previous chapters some of the habits which sustain or increase our energy. If you have mastered the five-a-day habit described in the previous chapter and you are generally getting the right amount of sleep, you will be well on the way to sustaining your energy levels. What can you do to make sure you are not overloading your energy circuits, or that when an energy surge is required, you have something in reserve?

If you have already completed the exercise in chapter one concerning what fosters and what undermines your emotional resilience and have not yet gone back to it, you may wish to do so now. Ask yourself which of the rewarding factors are also energising, and which of the undermining factors drain your energy. It is easy to say 'do more of one and less of the other' but somehow it is not quite that simple.

An experience that frequently drains our energy is a feeling of being overwhelmed by work. There is so much to do that we hardly know where to start. If that is your experience, it is worth focusing on how you are managing your workload.

Managing your workload

Almost everyone enjoys some part of their role more than others. A natural human reaction is to postpone activities that we enjoy less, or find challenging. Mark Twain is reported to have recommended that you should start each day by swallowing a frog; that way, you know that nothing worse is going to happen to you throughout the day.

How aware are you of your own 'frogs', the issues that you really would rather not be engaged in? Consider the activities that take your time throughout a working week, note down those you can remember at the end of the week, and rate them on a 1-10 scale. A score towards 10 means you find the activity enjoyable and easy to prioritise; a score nearer 1 indicates that you are less keen on the activity and are likely to prevaricate if it is not appropriate or possible to delegate it. This is a hypothetical example from a school as an illustration. Yours will look different.

Exercise 5: Understand your preferences to help manage your workload

Tasks	prevaricate		prioritise
1. Analysing data	1	——————————————┼————	10
2. Writing reports for governors	1	————————┼—————————	10
3. Attending conferences	1	———————————————┼———	10
4. Meeting senior colleagues	1	——————————————┼————	10
5. Walking the corridors	1	——————————┼————————	10
6. Lesson observations	1	————————————┼——————	10
7. etc	1	———————————————————	10

You may be well aware of the things you do and do not enjoy working on. The benefit of this exercise is that it allows you to rate one against another, so you can choose to engage with your 'frogs' (those things you are less keen on) at the time when you feel most able to do so. You would be wise to spread such activities during the week, and not to try to undertake them all at once, or if you have had a poor night's sleep, or are already feeling drained.

When you have completed your list, review those that you have scored towards 10. Be aware that some of the things that you look forward to most may not have a significant impact on your organisation. Consider carefully whether you are using them to distract you from those things that you are less inclined to embrace.

There are no right or wrong answers here. The idea is simply to help you to stop and consider what you find yourself doing that you may be able to delegate. Think about the skills, capacity and potential of those in your team. There may be someone who would not have the skills to undertake a particular role now, but with training would welcome the opportunity to do so. Coaching clients sometimes tell me that they are unable to delegate a role or responsibility, when actually what they mean is that they rather enjoy doing whatever it is, so they do not wish to give it away, or they do not trust anyone else to do it as well as they do.

An alternative way of reviewing your working patterns is to consider the degree to which your agenda is driven by what is of strategic significance to the organisation. When did you last consider with members of your team how responsibilities are distributed? When a new appointment is made, do you review the tasks across the team to ensure that individuals are using their strengths, or proactively building expertise in an area they wish to develop? What is your unique contribution to your organisation? What do you do which no one else could? If you were absent and no one took over the activities you engage in, what would the organisation miss? How long could your absence last without your organisation losing focus or direction? How much time do you spend on managerial tasks and which of those could you delegate to others? If you are someone who finds it difficult to let go and allow others to take over, you are very likely to find yourself feeling overwhelmed by having too much to do. There is little more guaranteed to drain your energy than a sense of not being in control of your own agenda. If you find yourself constantly reacting, rather than having the space to plan and implement your own agenda, it is time to stand back and take stock.

If you have ever tried to Skype someone on an inadequate internet connection that has constantly disconnected, or have had your favourite television programme interrupted when watching on your computer with the display 'sorry, you don't have enough bandwidth to play this right now' you will have an objective illustration of what is happening to your brain when you are trying to do too many things at once. You simply have insufficient 'cognitive bandwidth' (working memory) to be able to think through all the items that require attention. Add to that the fact that the part of the brain you are compromising is the prefrontal cortex, responsible for complex decision-making, planning and creative thinking, and you will see how easy it is to get into a vicious circle. You are too busy, so you make less helpful decisions, so you agree to undertake work when you already have more than you can deal with. A meeting that is cancelled at the last minute feels like a gift from the gods. The psychological effect of suddenly having space where there previously appeared to be none may well be greater than is merited by the amount you achieve in the two hours that you might otherwise have been at the meeting, fretting about the fact that you are wasting your time. I see many people in large group presentations managing the sense of having too much to do by half-listening to what is going on at the front of the room whilst catching up on emails. Thanks to the availability of always-on technology, doing several things at the same time has become a national pastime. What neuroscience tells us, however, is that we are in fact switching our attention rapidly from one activity to another, using greater energy than we would do if we focused on one thing at a time.

83

While you are taking stock, consider the following questions:

Question 1: What time of day am I most productive?

Some of us are larks, and some are owls – and some fall in between. Recognising the circumstances under which you do your best work will allow you to focus on the more difficult aspects when you are at your best.

Question 2: How often do I protect time for myself without interruptions?

An 'open door policy' that involves being constantly available if you are in school, is death to productive working. If you are constantly available to others, are you in danger of contributing to a culture of dependence? Many leaders I work with will work at home in order to be at their most productive. Some establish it as a helpful habit, setting aside time regularly; others have to get to screaming pitch before they feel justified in taking time away from school or the office; some I work with resist working at home altogether because they do not allow their own staff to do so, or because they worry that other people will think they are taking time off. You will make your own decision; just be aware of what lies behind it. When headteachers justify their constant availability by telling me they want to be approachable and available to staff, I sometimes want to ask whose needs they are serving.

Many years ago, I telephoned a colleague for some advice about how to tackle an issue with someone whom he knew better than I did. 'I don't want you to do it for me, George,' I said 'I just want to know what approach you think I should take'. 'Leave it with me' came the reply. 'I didn't want you to do it for me,' I reiterated 'I just wanted your advice'. 'You've asked for my advice' he said 'my advice is to leave it with me'. I did leave it with him, but I felt slightly frustrated, wondering whether he did not trust me to deal with the issue. Thanks to Kenneth Blanchard's *The One Minute Manager Meets the Monkey*,[37] the phenomenon of picking up other people's 'monkeys' is pretty well known, but it is not always easy to be aware of being a participant in this game unless we stop and review recent interactions. Think about the last week. How many people's

---

37   Blanchard, K. (2011): *The One Minute Manager Meets the Monkey*. London: Harper Collins.

difficulties did you hand back to them with encouragement to find a way forward, and how many did you pick up? Just like a parent who holds the bicycle seat of their child as they learn to ride, sometimes you need to let go, even if they might fall, in order to allow them to learn to ride without stabilisers. Questions, rather than answers, will help individuals to find their own solutions.

Emails are insidious. If we allow them to, they become like earworms, nagging at us, and diverting us from our own agenda. If I leave my email client open in the background when I am working on something else, I am constantly aware of emails pinging in to my in box, and I cannot avoid seeing the name of the sender and the first few words of the email. Even if I choose to ignore the email after that, the very fact that I have registered its arrival is sufficient to have taken my focus from the matter in hand. Reading it in full can take me off track altogether, as I make a decision regarding whether I am going to respond instantly or not. Maybe I need to look up something in order to be helpful to someone else. Before I know where I am, my morning's planning has been hijacked by leaving my inbox open. When I ask why I allow my own agenda to be hijacked in this way, I have to acknowledge it is partly out of habit – in the early days of consultancy I was always hoping that the next email would bring a commission.

I still value those emails, but I have learned that a moment's hesitation in responding is a good thing: it allows me to consider whether I have the time and the expertise to meet the demand. Then, of course, there is the dopamine rush to my brain, when I respond to (or indeed delete) an email and see the numbers in my inbox diminishing. That is a clear indication of how I have spent my morning. As I am strongly driven by a need to achieve, providing myself with tangible evidence of a productive morning is motivating.

Question 3: How often do I continue working when I am struggling to concentrate?

There is a difference between not allowing constant interruptions and working without interruption. If you have a lengthy demanding task to undertake, it is wise to build in some breaks in order to be able to sustain your levels of concentration. You will find your own rhythm, but if you spend three hours in front of a computer screen without a break, each hour is likely to be less productive than the one before. Set an alarm to remind you to get up and walk somewhere, to give your pre-frontal cortex space to recover before you ask more of it. Signs that you need a break include re-reading the same sentence several times without taking it in, checking emails, or checking something on the internet (a great distraction, but not a proper break). If you know you are tired, stop working.

If you were to insert an energy smart meter into your brain, you would find that the prefrontal cortex – the part of the brain responsible for executive function, often referred to as the PFC – is energy hungry. It operates at its best when it is well rested and when bouts of intense activity are interspersed with low-level activities, such as answering routine email. For maximum efficiency in using the PFC, it is a good idea to allow periods of respite between intense concentration on complex issues. How often have you struggled to complete, or indeed begin, something creative to find that if you leave and come back to it, suddenly things become clear? You might talk about 'taking a walk to clear my head'. It is akin to that moment when your computer suddenly decides to install new updates: it is fruitless to try to use it while the updates are installing. We also talk about 'sleeping on it' when we have something weighty to consider, which often results in greater clarity. When it is sleep deprived it is less able to make decisions which benefit our, and/or the organisation's long- and short-term interests. Indeed, in some cases our own interests or values may conflict with those of the organisation.

If any of the questions outlined above have caused you to consider amending your working patterns, you may need to develop some new habits of behaviour that will serve you better. Routine is helpful. It provides structure and prevents us from having to consider actions afresh. Imagine that all your activities in a single day – from attending a meeting to getting up and having breakfast, to answering emails, to cleaning your teeth, driving to work, dressing, washing and so on – were scrambled into any old order and that you spent time in bed in the morning trying to schedule them in a logical order. Not only could you easily arrive at work still in your night clothes, you would already have spent considerable time and energy before getting up, in deciding what to do first.

The focus of the UK government's biennial teacher workload survey on hours worked, signifies an implicit assumption that the longer our working hours, the more drained we feel. It is not just hours worked which drain our energy, however. There are other factors that need to be taken into account in undertaking our energy audit.

Question 4: Who drains my energy?

Sir Tim Brighouse – sometime leader of the London Challenge and a well-known writer on UK education – used to talk about radiators and drains in the staff room. The radiators are the enthusiasts who are always up for a challenge and greet each day as an opportunity to learn. The drains are the ones that sit in a huddle in the staffroom until the last possible moment when the bell goes; they mutter under their breath when a new idea is proffered at a staff meeting, and phrases such as 'that'll never work' and 'we tried that five years ago' are frequently heard to pass their lips. Leaders need to be eternally (though not unrealistically) optimistic if they are to win hearts and minds. On a day when things are not going well, it is easy to feel sucked down by the drains. Radiators give off warmth; their heat is your energy. In your professional life you may be unable to avoid the drains, but the more radiators you have, the greater the chance of the warmth reducing the damp of the drains.

Managing yourself in order to manage others

As a leader with ultimate responsibility for the outcomes of your organisation, you are consistently required to exercise a level of self-control rarely required of others. Regardless of the context in which you lead, whether in an orchestra, a school, a classroom, a department within a commercial organisation or as the CEO of a large conglomerate, if you are trying to achieve outcomes through others, you will need to manage your own behaviour in order to create the conditions for others to flourish. You have to place the good of the organisation above your personal impulses and needs, holding back instinctive reactions to, for example, a personal attack, balancing your desire to say exactly what you think with the long-term interests of you or the organisation. All of this has an impact on energy.

When working with groups of leaders, I have often asked them to talk about the behaviour of leaders that they have worked with, which they judge to have been effective. Whatever level of leadership within an organisation I have been working with, I have had similar responses. Comments include: 'encouraging, consistent, made us believe in ourselves, inspiring, walked the talk, honest, confident.' Conversely, the behaviour of leaders with whom people would not choose to work again is represented by such words as 'coercive, bullying, had favourites, kept changing her mind, scary, self-absorbed, uncaring, inconsistent, miserable'. I ask about the impact of that behaviour. Time and again what I hear confirms the truth of Maya Angelou's famous pronouncement: 'people will forget what you said, people will forget what you did, but people will never forget how you made them feel.'

If you are a school leader, you will immediately see the connection between leading a school and leading a classroom. In the late 1990s, I took part in a project by HayMcBer (now the Hay Group) who had been commissioned by the UK Department for Education to research into and identify a model of teacher effectiveness. They were particularly keen to test whether their model of leadership effectiveness for organisations resonated in classroom practice. Among the three factors within a teacher's control that were identified as having an impact on pupils' progress was classroom climate – 'the collective perceptions by pupils of what it feels like to be a pupil in any particular teacher's classroom, where those perceptions influence every student's motivation to learn and perform to the best of his or her ability.'[38] In much the same way as the leader in an organisation creates the motivational climate for the workers, so a teacher in a classroom, given similar technical skills, will have a greater or lesser impact on pupils' performance through the classroom climate created.

You are accountable for the outcomes of your organisation but you are not wholly responsible. In fact, difficult though this may be to live with, you cannot make anyone do anything. You can only increase or decrease the likelihood of them taking action through the conditions you create as a leader. Leaders at every level in an organisation are called on to use their energy to create the emotional climate that motivates others to achieve the organisation's vision. In any interaction with others, much of our behaviour is automatic; some may require a significant amount of self-management. When someone asks you 'what did you think of my presentation?' you have to think carefully how you deliver the message so that it will be heard in the way you mean it to be heard. The newer you are to a role, the more energy this self-management is likely to take; you are conscious that individuals will be watching every move as they try to work out who you are and what you stand for. Getting to know your team and building trust take time. Once trust is established, if you are having a bad day and respond with irritation in a meeting, for example, people may look at each other with some surprise, and it will be forgotten. A similar response early in your tenure will be interpreted as indicative of your way of operating. The exercise of self-control saps energy.

Exercising willpower

Thanks to Walter Mischel's famous 'marshmallow test'[39], which tested children's ability to exercise self-control in the interests of delayed gratification, we know that some children appear to be more able to exercise self-control than others of the same age, so some of us have a head start on being able to exercise self-control. Whatever your starting point, however, self-control can be developed. Before Suzanne Segerstrom's

---

38   Hay McBer. (2000): *Research into Teacher Effectiveness*. London: DfEE.
39   Mischel, W. (2014): *The Marshmallow Test*. Transworld Publishers.

work, cited in chapter two, Roy Baumeister also described willpower as being like a muscle that can be strengthened with practice, and can also become exhausted even though we may not be aware that it is running out.[40] Most of us find it harder to push ourselves to do things we would rather not do when we are tired. There is good reason for this, in that exercising willpower actually demands more of our bodies than we might imagine. We are used to the idea that feeling fear has an impact on our bodies: increased heart rate, elevated cortisol levels, faster breathing, are all triggered by our fight or flight response to fear. The exercise of willpower, it turns out, gives rise to similar physiological changes and depletes blood glucose, which is necessary for effective functioning of the brain. If you are on a diet that demands that you resist sugary snacks, you had better make sure that you also maintain relatively stable blood sugar levels, because when they dip, your willpower dips with them. Regular exercise also helps your body to use glucose efficiently so by connection, willpower is stronger if you take regular exercise. The fact that actually undertaking the exercise may also call for you to 'exercise' willpower is a double benefit. If willpower can be likened to a muscle, then exercising it will make it strong.

Exercising willpower is one of the hidden ways in which leaders will be using their energy, as they manage their responses to hundreds of interactions with others. Just as our brains would be overloaded if we had to think consciously about every physical action we took during the day ('I must now put two feet on the ground, shift my weight forward, straighten my legs, and move one foot after another', for example) so if we consciously managed every single interaction with others, we would undoubtedly be in the position of cognitive overload, and be unable to function. Repeated actions or responses helpfully lead to neural connections in the brain that, over time, become embedded habits. We no longer need to think about them. When something is embedded as a habit, it demands little willpower. Some of our habits will be helpful in our current role, and some of them not.

---

40   Baumeister, R. F. (2003): Ego depletion and self-regulation failure. *Clinicial and Experiemental Research*, 27 (2), pp. 281-84.

Emotional labour

Leadership demands emotional engagement. The act of managing our emotions takes energy. Scientists frequently refer it to as 'emotional labour'. Emotional labour occurs when an individual is required to subjugate their genuine emotions in order to display emotions that are consistent with expectations (whether written, understood, or self-imposed). Researchers in Australia studied 1320 school principals in order to investigate the impact of emotional labour on their job satisfaction, wellbeing and burnout.[41] They looked in particular at three aspects of behaviour, which have been used by researchers to characterise emotional labour:

- Surface acting (faking)
- Surface acting (hiding)
- Deep acting

Whatever organisation you work in, if you have a client or customer-facing role, you will know the pressures of surface acting. Cold callers, for example, often start their script with 'how are you today?' although recipients of these calls may be fairly sure that it is not a genuine inquiry. Checkout operators are required to smile and remain positive regardless of the response they encounter. Surface acting (faking) is when we behave as though we were experiencing an emotion when we are not. For example, an influential board member who is constantly criticising your way of working appears in your office at the worst possible moment. 'Good to see you,' you say through metaphorically gritted teeth, with a smile that you hope does not appear as false as it feels. You might behave in this way for a variety of reasons: out of fear, to minimise the possibility of yet more negative criticism, or because you know that this is someone you are going to have to get on with whether you like it or not; or, for many other reasons.

The leaders referred to at the opening of this book exemplify surface acting (hiding). They acted as though they were confident while in reality they feared that they would be exposed as being not up to the job.

---

41   Maxwell, A. & Riley, P. (2017): Emotional demands, emotional labour and occupational outcomes in school principals. *Educational management, administration and leadership*, pp. 484-502.

If you are required to implement a policy you do not fully agree with, you may find yourself surface acting (hiding) in order to convince others that it will work. If your company is facing financial difficulties you might choose to hide this from your employees and pretend all is well, so as not to worry them, or not to prompt a mass exodus from the organisation that will certainly ensure its demise. As leaders we must constantly check our level of honesty to gauge whether it is in the organisation's best interests.

It is 1998, and the end of my first day delivering on a national leadership programme. I have gone to my room and shut the door on what has been very a challenging day. I have never done anything like this before, except in training. I have never been good at being the centre of attention and I have had to stand up in front of a group of people who have delivered training professionally for many years. I feel every eye on me as I explain the theory of the programme. I am trying to remain positive, but I feel anything but. I compare myself with my partner – an experienced educator from a university – and feel sure that everyone is making the same comparison, saying to each other in private, 'whatever is she doing here?' Surely it can be only a matter of time before someone says it out loud, and (although they will be expressing a sentiment I agree with) I shall not know what to say. I find myself less and less able to engage with individuals, as though to interact with someone is likely to open up the opportunity for them to express their misgivings about my performance. As so often when I need someone to listen, I telephone my sister in order to share my anxieties. I have no idea how I'm going to keep going. If I'm not actually crying, my voice is certainly shaky and she can be in no doubt about my emotional state. 'Now then,' she says, assertively, as the conversation comes to an end, 'you can do it, just stop worrying about what everybody's thinking and focus on what you're good at: imagining how they might be feeling and building relationships.'

Neither she nor I knew at the time that what she was advocating was 'deep acting'. Deep acting is required when helpful emotions – though not instinctive – are deliberately and authentically engaged, requiring a certain amount of cognitive effort to focus on the underlying issues.

For example, if you notice yourself becoming irritated by a worker who is consistently resisting change and you know that there are significant challenges in his or her personal life, you might deliberately choose to focus on what a tough time the individual is having personally, in order to replace irritation with compassion and understanding. Because you are now genuinely feeling those emotions, you will change your tone and the words you choose to use to ones that are more likely to gain a positive response from the employee. To engage in surface acting in this situation would require only that you smiled and tried hard to keep the irritation out of your voice.

The results of the study of school principals referred to above suggest that they are faced with higher emotional demands than the general population and that, despite the attributes that we would normally associate with wellbeing (defined in the study as secure employment, favourable salary and stable family relationships) their wellbeing is judged as being poorer than that of the general population. It was found that surface acting (hiding) was correlated with lower job satisfaction, poorer wellbeing and greater likelihood of burnout. Surface acting (faking) was related to lower job satisfaction only. So hiding your emotions appears to have a greater negative impact on your wellbeing than faking them. Deep acting appeared to have no significant impact on wellbeing, job satisfaction, or burnout. In fact in another study, where the amount of deep acting exceeded surface acting, this was related to a reduction in emotional exhaustion up to a year later.[42] Hiding emotion was the strategy used most often, and one that, in preventing principals from being able to operate as their authentic selves, is most likely to lead to stress. Accepting that it will never be possible to eliminate acting altogether from this type of role, the authors recommend deep acting as the most helpful approach to emotional labour.

You are alone in the first class carriage of a train. A man joins the carriage. He has two young children with him: you assess their ages at about four and seven. In an attempt to prove that you do not mind being disturbed in your carriage, which actually is untrue, you half-smile at the children. You

---

42   Schüpbach, A. P. (2010): Longitudinal effects of emotional labour on emotional exhaustion and dedication of teachers. *Journal of Occupational Health Psychology*, 15 (4), pp. 494-504.

are reading and commenting on material that has just arrived by email and needs to be returned by the end of the day. One of them takes this as a signal that you want a conversation, and begins to ask you questions about your computer. You answer as politely as you can, wishing all the time that their father – which you assume the man to be – would engage them in conversation himself and leave you in peace. You resort to frowning darkly, hoping that the child will take the hint that you do not wish to be disturbed. The children then start a game of hide and seek around the empty seats, giggling as they run and hide from each other. Through all this, the man seems oblivious to their behaviour and the fact that you are being disturbed. You spend some time trying to formulate words that sound polite but assertive and eventually say to the man 'Do you think you could possibly restrain your children a little? I'm finding it very difficult to concentrate on my work'. The man looks up, as though aware of you and the children for the first time. 'I'm so sorry,' he says. 'I was so deep in thought that I didn't even notice. You see, the children's mother – my daughter – died recently and we're returning from her funeral. I don't want to be too hard on the children. They have had enough to contend with today.'

Immediately you re-appraise the situation and your attitude changes; your response is now driven by compassion, as you hesitantly offer your condolences.

We do not need people to tell us their life story in order to be able to approach them with compassion. None of us knows the full detail of anyone else's story that has contributed to any given set of circumstances. We can, however, make up one that will change our emotional response. Perhaps there is a colleague you want to shake to bring her back to reason, because she is behaving like a spoiled child. Somewhere within her that child still exists. If you see before you a vulnerable child rather than an obstructive adult, you may be able to manage your response differently.

Exercise 6: Build compassion through imaginative understanding

Bring to mind someone you find it difficult to interact with. As objectively and accurately as you can, make a list of the aspects of their behaviour that you find challenging. Remember no one can make you feel anything and describe the facts, not the effect of their behaviour. Now put the person out of your mind, and review the list. Invent a story about this person's upbringing that allows you to track their current behaviour to something they lacked in childhood. For example, someone who drives you mad because they are always interrupting your day to seek your approval may have been constantly criticised as a child. Someone that constantly contradicts you in public may have been dominated by an overbearing parent – probably of the same gender as you. Someone who bursts into tears when you criticise their performance may have learned to avoid the consequences of their actions by doing so as a child.

Now review the list again. Is there anything here that you, as a leader, should have challenged? Have you shared the impact of their behaviour with them? Do you ever think 'I shouldn't need to tell them'? If the fact is that you do, simply wishing things were different is a waste of energy and you carry an unnecessary (and energy-consuming) burden of resentment.

We cannot like equally everyone we work with. Given they are competent at their job (and if they are not, you will need to speak to their line manager about their improvement) consider what it would cost you to put down the anger, irritation or resentment that you feel, and which is needlessly consuming your energy. And remember, no one can make you feel inferior without your consent.

Deep acting – deliberately engaging a desired emotion rather than just hiding the one you are really feeling – does not mean excusing inappropriate behaviour from others. What it does mean is that you are more likely to respond than to react to a situation, because you have gone one step further than hiding your feelings with a mask of tolerance. You will have engaged with an emotion that is likely to influence your response in a way that is helpful to your long-term interests. Deep acting is likely to consume less energy than surface acting, and leads to less stress. The more authentically you can act, however, the less energy you will consume in emotional labour.

Channelling your energy

When I ask workshop participants how we use our energy unproductively, one word that I always hear is 'worry'. In *The 7 Habits of Highly Effective People*[43] Stephen Covey talks about circle of influence and circle of concern, pointing out that when we concern ourselves with matters outside our circle of influence and focus on things we can do nothing about, negative energy results. I do not know whether Covey knew the work of American theologian, Reinhold Niebuhr, but a similar sentiment exists in the well-known 'serenity prayer', which asks for 'help to accept the things I cannot change, the courage to change the things I can, and the wisdom to know the difference'.

We are served best when our short-term priorities serve our long-term needs. That is the challenge. On a very basic level, do I deny myself that short-term need to eat a bar of chocolate in order to look and feel better

---

43   Covey, S. (1989): *The 7 Habits of Highly-Effective People*. London: Simon & Schuster.

about myself when I put on my bikini on the beach in four months' time? As a leader, do I avoid dealing with the less than satisfactory performance by a member of staff because I know it will be disruptive and cause unrest amongst the staff? I have been party to many instances in schools where issues have been left in order to avoid rocking the boat. While this will conserve energy in the short term, it is important that the decision is made consciously considering the gains and losses of tackling something immediately as against waiting for it to improve without intervention.

Before the conductor described at the opening of this chapter engaged in activity with his orchestra, he certainly spent time silently studying the orchestral score. One of his areas of focus would have been where to direct his attention at any given time. It would not have been productive use of his energy if he had focused on the horns throughout the first movement, if they were due to play for only the last 28 bars. If he focused solely on the strings, who were playing most of the time, and never thought about the atmosphere he wanted to create when the horns made their entry, he would not have achieved his long-term aim. Without taking the time to study the score and plan where to focus his attention at any time, he would have been trying to make such decisions in the moment. Easily distracted by what was in his immediate environment (generally, the strings) he might easily have forgotten to direct the horns, who were due to play for only that last 28 bars.

We, too, need to pause and reflect on our priorities. It is when we find ourselves too busy to pause that things get out of balance. When we invest too much of ourselves in work, there is nothing left to nourish the relationships and activities outside of work that keep us going. Whether in leadership or in life, we all need to find the right balance between immediate and long-term professional and personal priorities in order to achieve success. It is easy to say, and it will probably not come as a surprise to you. The surprising thing is how difficult it is to do, even when we know it is a helpful habit to develop, and have every intention of ensuring that we take time out to reflect. Like all habits, it is cost-free once in place and the benefits are considerable.

Worth remembering

- We become less efficient when we have too many simultaneous priorities; we simply have insufficient cognitive bandwidth.
- We can influence others only through our own behaviour.
- When behaviour becomes habitual, it demands less energy.
- If we hide our true feelings, we may be using more energy than we need to in managing our emotional responses to a situation.
- We need to protect time to be able to stand back and focus on strategic issues.
- For maximum efficiency and effectiveness we need to align short and long-term professional and personal priorities and plans.

Chapter Four:
Agency

There are about 12 of us in the room. On the cards in front of us are pictures of different creatures. We are invited to select two and introduce ourselves as the creatures we have selected. I have chosen a dolphin and an ant. It is easy to think of reasons to be attracted to a dolphin: it is intelligent, streamlined, well adapted to its environment, and popular. As I look at the picture of the ant I am taken back to an episode 40 years earlier when I was a child. We were living in the Middle East and returned from an evening out to find an army of ants marching at least three abreast across the kitchen floor, up the cupboards, on to the surfaces, up the wall and in to a cupboard, where a jar of jam revealed itself as the focus of interest. Someone had returned it to the cupboard without ensuring the removal of every last vestige of jam that might have dripped on to the outside of the jar. Sitting with the group on this counselling training residential programme, I am struck by the persistence and dogged determination of the ants to reach their destination. In my family such behaviour is greatly valued (when not applied to ants in the kitchen). Yet, I also recognise that keeping on keeping on without ever questioning whether it is the right thing to do, or whether there could be a different way to be, has made my life very challenging in recent times.

Nearly 20 years have passed since I sat in that room. From my more recent experience of coaching, I know that I was not alone in finding it difficult to stand still, take stock and change my behaviour. If you had given me a list of words to choose from on that day, rather than shown me pictures, I wonder whether my choice would have been the same. The moment we think in words, we engage in cognitive processing. We think of ourselves as rational beings with the capacity to choose our behaviour, and yet much of what we considered in the last chapter consisted of our working against our best interests, which is hardly logical.

If we want to sustain our resilience, we need to do more of what sustains us, and less of what undermines us. It sounds simple. We might have a good understanding of the theory, but putting that into action can be far, far more demanding than we might appreciate. Viktor Frankl talks about the last human freedom being our right to choose.[44] He does not talk about our capacity to choose. If we are to change how we live our lives, we need a strong sense of agency.

According to the Oxford English Dictionary, an 'agent' is 'a person or thing that takes an active role or produces a particular effect'. So we need not just the freedom to choose, but also the capacity, which includes a belief in our ability to have a 'particular effect'. If you open the cage door of a bird that is physically able to fly but believes it cannot fly, it will remain captive. Without the belief in our own ability to have an effect, we negate the capacity to choose, and the freedom is worthless. We are all capable of remaining captive to habits of thinking and behaviour that we have outgrown without even being aware of the impact of those habits on our daily lives. It is our sense of agency that translates the freedom to choose into action.

The importance of noticing

In *The Essential Enneagram*[45] David Daniels and Virginia Price refer to the four A's model of change: the stages are Awareness, Acceptance, Action and Adherence. We have no chance of taking remedial action if we are unaware of the potential for change or its possible benefits. We need consciously to take control of our own agenda. We must pay attention and develop our awareness of the messages our bodies and minds are sending, which impact on our habits of behaviour and thinking. Developing awareness calls you to bring into consciousness something of which you were previously unconscious. For example,

---

44   Frankl, V. E. (2004): *Man's Search for Meaning*. London: Ebury Press, Random House.
45   Daniels, D. N. & Price, V. A. (2009): *The Essential Enneagram*. New York: HarperCollins.

you may be unaware of a ticking clock in the room, until you try to go to sleep. You were previously unconscious of the noise, and it suddenly breaks into your consciousness.

The difference between that, and developing a habit of awareness, is that developing the habit allows you to determine for yourself when you will notice something of which you were previously not conscious. It is all about intentional focus. You could compare it to the process of focused listening, which you might do if you were walking in the countryside and thought you heard a cuckoo. You would probably stop and listen intently, and this focused listening would allow you to distinguish the sound of the cuckoo from that of other birds, the distant sound of traffic, and so on. There are lots of different ways of developing a habit of awareness. Practising mindfulness certainly helps. A brief introduction to how to start practising physical awareness is below.

Exercise 7: Developing a habit of awareness[46]

Find a space where you will not be interrupted – initially for five minutes or so. Whether you are standing, sitting or lying down, let your attention focus on the sensations in your body. Start by bringing into your awareness that most automatic of habits: your breathing. Notice the movement of the air through your nose, and down into your lungs. Notice where your breath is coming from; notice the movement of your chest and abdomen as you inhale and exhale. There is no need to change your breathing, simply notice what is happening. You will almost certainly find that your attention wanders away from your breath, to something in the future, or an event that has happened. When you notice that you are no longer focusing on your breathing, gently allow your breathing to come back into focus. Can you feel any tension in your face? How is your jaw? Are you clenching your teeth, or is it relaxed? Are you holding your tongue in a certain position, or is it resting gently on the roof of your mouth? What about your shoulders? Are they hunched or relaxed? Move your attention down your arms and notice the sensations there. Focus your attention on your hands. Notice your breathing. Is it quick and shallow or deep and long? What else do you notice?

---

46 I regard mindfulness and awareness as related. Practising mindfulness allows us to develop awareness and goes beyond it, to encourage non-judgemental acceptance of those things of which we become aware.

> Now allow your attention to focus on the sensations in your body. Starting with your feet, scan gently from your toes and feet, up your legs, your torso, your arms and shoulders, neck, face, including your jaw and forehead, and up into your hairline. Go slowly, giving yourself time to feel anything there is to feel. When you find yourself being distracted by thought, just re-focus and allow your attention to rest on your body again. Switch back, then, to focusing on your breath. After whatever time period you have allocated (I often set a timer) pause before you carry on with whatever now needs to occupy your focus, and congratulate yourself on giving yourself the gift of time.

Practise this or another exercise (there are many on the internet) as often as you can – preferably daily, working up to ten minutes a day. Try not to think of it as something that you are trying to improve. It is the practice itself that is beneficial. The moment you think of it as something you want to get better at, you are introducing an element of judgement, which is likely to precipitate negative thoughts.

As you develop a habit of awareness and become more aware of the messages your body is communicating, you will also become more aware of how you are feeling emotionally.

'What is it that you'd like to focus on today?' I am used to my client being someone who understands his position by talking about it aloud. Even for him, there follows an unusually long monologue as he describes one thing and then another, circling round an issue, coming back, revisiting and leaving it, only to return again leaving off in mid-sentence to explore another avenue. I am beginning to feel lost and overwhelmed, mirroring exactly what my client is feeling. 'Would it be helpful to get some of these things on the table?' I ask. 15 minutes later he is surrounded by a confetti of post-it notes and the remainder of the session focuses on how he will group and prioritise them. When I leave he tells me the session has been helpful and I believe him. Several weeks later, when I see him again, it emerges that he has been off work, suffering with illness that I, at least, attribute to stress.

Now, several years later, and much more aware of the connection between physical, mental and emotional wellbeing, I like to think that I might respond somewhat differently to such a situation, paying greater attention to my client's mental health and wellbeing and focusing less on asking him to exercise his decision-making function. We might have had a 'walking coaching' session in the fresh air, to change the environment. I might have asked him about his sleep patterns, or when he last had time off, or away from the office.

It is very easy to imagine that a diagnosis of stress will never happen to us; just in case we are wrong, we avoid seeking help that might confirm our worst fears. What would prompt you to decide that you might need additional support to deal with the stresses of your role? We all know stories of a patient who puts off visiting the doctor because he or she does not have time, or for fear of the diagnosis (or both) before finally being told that if she had come earlier the prognosis would be less serious. We need to pay attention to the early warning signs of stress and reach out before we have lost the capacity to do so. Stress and depression rob us of our agency; we cease to act rationally, driven by unmediated emotion.

Acceptance

There are all sorts of things that get in the way of our accepting uncomfortable truths, both as leaders and as individuals. We do not have to go very far to remind ourselves of institutional blindness that has allowed sexual exploitation of the vulnerable. How do you know that the climate you intend to create is what others experience in the organisation you are leading? How do you know that you are not being told what others think you want to hear in order to protect their own position?

If we want to build resilience, and that means changing some of our habits, how able are we to accept the need for change? Does it require accepting an unpalatable truth? James Hilton, the headteacher referred to in chapter one, ignored the signs of creeping stress and pressure until he became unable to function. We all have an image of ourselves and when something happens to challenge that image, it is hard to accept. Consider this sentence:

'I see myself as _____'

Complete it with whatever characteristic or skill is important to you, either professionally or personally, or both. For me it might read, 'I see myself as a good facilitator.' When I am facilitating, I strive to ask open questions and encourage everyone to contribute to discussions. I generally think of myself as an effective facilitator. When I had been working with a new group and received feedback via a third party that I was perceived to have 'closed down the debate', my first response was 'that's not me'. I had to find a way of accommodating what appeared to be mutually exclusive truths: 'I am a skilled facilitator' and 'I have closed down debate inappropriately.' Which of these could I most easily believe? I had to ask myself whether it had to be 'either or'. Could it be 'both and', accepting that the other person's perception is their reality and that this one piece of feedback did not necessarily negate all the positive feedback I had had over the years?

Changing habits that no longer serve us may mean questioning 'truths' that have been handed to us by our parents: 'big boys don't cry', for example, or 'always put others first'. If we are to change habits of thinking and behaving, we may have to distinguish our own beliefs from those that have been handed to us by others in our lives. That can be a painful and challenging experience. It is also necessary if we are to develop our own autonomy, rather than being the agent of our family or organisational system.

Action: Establishing helpful habits

Just as starting something new takes energy, so does stopping. In chapter two we focused on changes in behaviour that would increase energy. In chapter three we considered how everyday interactions might drain that energy. Replacing unhelpful habits (such as overwork, worry, omnipotent thinking) with helpful ones requires conscious effort and self-control until the new habit is established. As we have seen above, self-control, or willpower takes energy. In order to be able to operate as effectively and efficiently as possible, you will need to establish habits of behaviour and thinking which serve your best interests. Since to be a leader is to be an agent of change, changing habits is something leaders are used to working on. In many cases, however, the habits leaders work hard to change are those of others.

Only when a particular behaviour becomes habitual are we able to stop making a conscious effort to enact it. The focus on teachers' wellbeing has increased considerably in recent years. In 2014 the UK government launched the workload challenge, a nationwide survey that asked teachers for their views concerning unnecessary workload and pledged to conduct a similar survey every two years thereafter. From the 1st of September 2017, the UK schools' inspectorate, Ofsted, was charged with asking headteachers routinely what they are doing to reduce teachers' workload. In 2003 there was an attempt to relieve workload pressure on headteachers with the Workload Agreement.[47] Amongst its aims was to ensure better work-life balance, making provision for 'dedicated headship time'. However, over half of the 3000 headteachers who took part in the NAHT survey in 2008-2009 did not take advantage of this provision.[48]

---

47 ATL, DfES, GMB, NAHT, NASUWT, NEOST, PAT, et al. (2003): *Raising Standards and Tackling Workload*. Available at: http://dera.ioe.ac.uk/540/1/081210thenationalagreementen. pdf

48 French, S. (2009): *The NAHT Worklife Balance Survey 2008-2009*. Available at: www.naht.org. uk

It is 2009 and at the leadership festival the workshop on developing emotional resilience for leadership is full, with some having not managed to sign up in time to gain a place. After the usual discussions concerning what supports and what undermines resilience; how there is never enough time; and the difficulty of stopping to breathe and take stock, I tentatively ask how many people in the room make space for themselves by prioritising professional coaching. I am cautious because – as a professional coach – I am aware of the danger of 'coat trailing'. Coaching is not the only way to protect time for yourself, but it is considerably more effective, in my experience, than putting a line through a page in a diary and vowing you will keep it for yourself – until something more urgent comes along. Among the audience of 20 or so, a couple of hands are raised. 'I used to,' offers someone else. 'Yes,' comments another, 'we used to get money which we had to spend on coaching and things'. 'That's right,' suggests a third voice. 'If we had money especially for it, I'd spend it'. I feel both frustrated and sympathetic. I know that these headteachers want to do the best for their students and that spending money on themselves feels like an indulgence. At the same time, I am impatient at their short-sightedness. 'Oh that's interesting,' I say, managing, I think, to keep the frustration out of my voice. 'Who in your school manages the budget?'

Governors certainly have a role to play here. They should be aware of their headteachers' response to pressure of work. On the other hand, as we have already noted, no one can make anyone else do anything. As the leader you and you alone, have to develop the healthy autonomy that allows you to take control and work to sustain your resilience. It takes time and commitment. Sustaining resilience is not an action, it is a way of living, and for most of us, it will involve many setbacks and failures to keep resolutions, but it feeds on itself. You cannot leave it to someone else. With each step towards building a helpful habit, your resilience grows. With increased resilience comes an increased capacity for making decisions that sustain resilience and for keeping going in the face of setbacks.

Schools rightly focus on the experience of the children and young people they exist to serve. Headteachers I have worked with constantly put others first. This is borne out by the results of my masters survey already referred to, which revealed that headteachers spent more time focusing on the emotional resilience of pupils and staff, than on their own. Eight out of ten said they paid significant attention to that of pupils, six out of ten paid attention to the emotional resilience of the staff, while fewer than half spent time focusing on their own emotional resilience in the same way.

In swimming lessons at school I trained for my bronze medallion in lifesaving. I am not sure that I would be capable of saving anyone from drowning by jumping in to the water these days, but I do recall the constant reinforcement of the message that if we came across someone in difficulty in the water the last thing (literally) we should do was to jump in to save them. This should be the last resort, when all other options had been considered and rejected as impractical. First we were told to consider other options, such as throwing a lifebelt, or a rope, or holding out a pole, or jumping in to a boat. In this context, it seems obvious: if I were to jump in and also get into difficulties, there would be two people to rescue. Leaders need to support others as well as being conscious of the possible impact on their own survival. This is not selfishness but prudence. If the leader jumps overboard to save a drowning crew member and also drowns, there will be no one to steer the ship through the rocky waters.

Helpful habit #1: Look after yourself

There is a difference, of course, between putting yourself in danger and finding something inconvenient. To stay late at work for meetings, for the most part, is an inconvenience. To stay late at school or the office night after night; to miss your evening meal every night and instead survive on crisps, chocolate and strong coffee; mentally or physical to bring your work home with you so that you have difficulty sleeping: such habits put not only yourself in danger, but your organisation too. Exhausted, you make less and less appropriate decisions, and work less efficiently. Our bodies are generally pretty tolerant of all we put them through, but after too long neglecting their needs, they will eventually send a strong message that all is not well. Returning from some time away from work suffering from stress, a leader explained to me how he had ignored the warning signs of increased migraines, poor sleep patterns during the week and binge sleeping at the weekends. Just like James Hilton, mentioned earlier in this book, and several other leaders I have worked with, he could see the signs only in retrospect.

In my front garden, adjacent to the path that leads to the front door is a fig tree. It is special to me because it was planted the year of my father's death, in his memory. I notice it every time I approach the front door. This year it has many figs on it, but they are not ripening. When I pass, I scrutinise it, hoping that one of the figs will have ripened since I last looked. A little further away from the front path is a gooseberry bush, which is equally special because my son gave it to me. I cannot see it from the path and I had no idea that it was becoming overrun with bindweed until one fine day when I told myself it was time I did some gardening (not something that happens all that often). It has had no flowers or fruit on it this year. I have neglected it. If only it were visible from the path, I might have noticed. Because I had to make a conscious effort to notice it, it has been neglected.

Many of us walk the path of life without noticing the messages our bodies are giving us until, like my gooseberry bush, they are overgrown with weeds. In order to maintain our energy levels, we need to notice daily how we are. That is a challenge for busy people who are distracted by busy minds that take over our physical bodies. We find ourselves in the house without being able to remember walking up the path. How often have you driven to work with no memory of significant parts of the journey, or even suddenly come to awareness on a journey and for a fraction of a second, do not recognise where you are? The first step is to notice.

> *Helpful habit #2: Pay attention to your wellbeing daily – when you notice the weeds, spend a little time refreshing the garden*

In chapter one I referred to my own experience of undertaking the eight-week mindfulness-based stress-reduction programme. Prior to attending I found it very difficult to notice a particular sensation. Following 16 hours of teaching and regular practice at home, I did become more able to focus on the sensations in my body. As a reminder, mindfulness is defined as paying attention, on purpose, in the present moment, non-judgementally. It can be applied to any activity: from cleaning your teeth to washing the dishes, as you consciously pay attention to what you are doing, rather than thinking about something else. The more you practise, the more able you are to control your focus, instead of letting your mind take control. There are all sorts of ways to help you to remember to pause and pay attention, from apps for your smartphone, to reminders on your computer or placing something prominently on your desk that is designed to remind you to pause. If you want to extend your practice and find it easier to do so when listening to spoken guidance, you can find numerous 'scripts' on the internet.

I am increasingly finding schools that have instituted mindfulness meditation practices for their students. A few consciously use the same practice with staff. I have yet to come across one where the leadership team practises mindfulness together as part of their regular routine.

Why mindfulness?[49]

Stopping to notice our physical sensations and taking action to look after our own physical wellbeing is one step towards sustaining emotional resilience. If sustaining emotional resilience allows us to experience

---

49   Mindfulness and awareness are often used to describe the same activity. I regard mindfulness as being characterised by Jon Kabat-Zinn's definition: paying attention, on purpose, in the present moment, non-judgementally. Awareness grows as a result of mindfulness, but awareness does not result in the non-judgemental response, which Jon Kabat-Zinn refers to.

emotion without being overwhelmed, it may be helpful to consider what happens physically when we become overwhelmed by emotion and how practising mindfulness or another form of awareness can help.

Although we may think of an emotion as something that is closely linked to mental wellbeing, an emotion is firstly a physical sensation caused by chemical changes in the brain. It is easy to forget that you do not have to verbalise something, or even to think, to experience it.

The brain has developed over millions of years. You can use your own hand to represent its development. Look at your wrist where it joins your arm and your hand, you can think of this as the brain stem. This is the most primitive part of the brain, sometimes referred to as the reptilian brain, pointing to our early existence as reptile-like creatures. Its function is to keep us alive and the behaviour it prompts is instinctive, rather than reasoned or learned. It regulates automatic life sustaining functions, such as the operation of the heart, lungs, temperature and so on, keeping our various functions in a relatively stable state when affected by external stimuli. It reacts to danger, instinctively prompting the fight, flight or freeze response.

If you then place your thumb into the palm of the same hand, with your fingers outstretched, you have a representation of the limbic, or mammalian brain, which includes the amygdala and hippocampus. It mediates the reptilian fight/flight/freeze response based on our previous experience. Put simply, the first time you encounter something that is perceived as threatening it gets filed away in your memory bank (the hippocampus). The next time you encounter the same event, the amygdala alerts you to the possible threat, sends a message to the hippocampus saying 'look out'; the hippocampus checks its files and says either 'it's okay; we've seen this before and it isn't dangerous', or 'you're right: engage high alert function', which is to send a message to the reptilian brain to increase heart rate, blood flow to the vital organs and blood sugar levels, to prime the body for action. These are all the bodily changes we experience when we are suddenly in danger. Mammals give birth to live young that have to be protected and nurtured if they are to survive. The mammalian brain is responsible for our nurturing instinct and distinguishes us from reptiles in that it enables the experience of a wide range of emotion.

Now bring your outstretched fingers over your thumb to make a fist and your fingers represent the most recent development of the human brain: the neocortex. It is responsible for many human characteristics, including our ability to reason and our capacity for creativity. The neocortex in a newborn baby is very small; most of the baby's functioning is about attending to its survival and emotional needs. It cries as a means of communicating; its brain has not developed sufficiently to be able to recognise that it is a separate being from its mother, or that crying may be regarded by its parents as an unwelcome intrusion. However, the neural pathways of a baby who is constantly neglected when it cries for help never develop as nature intended. Ultimately it will cease to communicate its need for attention.

As adults, our reptilian brain continues to perform the functions needed for survival. When we perceive danger, for example a narrow miss of another car on the motorway, we take evasive action instinctively. We may describe the feeling as 'my heart missed a beat' or 'my stomach lurched'. These are manifestations of the chemical messages being flashed round the brain by the autonomic nervous system that controls both the sympathetic (on switch) and the parasympathetic (off switch) nervous system. The chemical responses prepare the body to react to the danger: fight/flight or freeze. You may even find that you react in the same way if you think you see a car in the outside lane when you are about to pull out. Your amygdala and hippocampus do not get involved in calculating whether there was a car there last time you looked in your mirror. It is an instinctive reaction, even if it turns out to have been a trick of the light and not another car at all. There is a clear link here between external events, the brain and the body. Because we do not have time to think about the danger, it is more usual to regard the activity as brain-based, rather than mind-based.

In your daily life as a leader it is unlikely that you habitually feel that your life is in danger – unless you are on the front line in a role that routinely puts you in danger, of course. However, there are numerous opportunities for you to feel under threat, which will be linked to how you interpret what is going on around you. Your unconscious reaction to threat is very similar to the fight or flight response. When you perceive that you are under threat, your body demands increased glucose and oxygen and, just as in the fight/flight response, the release of cortisol is triggered. If not turned off by the parasympathetic nervous system when the threat has passed, an excess of cortisol over time results in decreased immunity, impaired liver function, and increased abdominal fat. Because the brain is busy dealing with the perceived threat, there is less capacity for reasoning, creative thinking or short-term memory recall.

Our working environments are complex and the relationship of the leader to the organisation is a little like that of the brain to the body. The leader is responsible for negotiating the various threats to the organisation that may come from a fluctuating stock market, aggressive competitors, maintaining a stable staff, for example. In schools threats might result from decreased budget and/or a falling roll, an Ofsted inspection, or an inability to recruit or retain good teachers. Since your job as a leader is to anticipate threat in order to remain on your chosen course, your role demands that you are on constant alert to threat. The more closely you identify with your organisation, the more personally you will feel the threat. In the model of the brain you have just constructed, you will notice the proximity to the neocortex of the mammalian brain (the thumb), which includes the amygdala. When the amygdala is activated by threat, it inevitably disturbs the functioning of the neocortex. One of the benefits of mindfulness meditation is its impact on the amygdala, which has been shown to be less easily aroused and to return to normal more quickly in the brains of those who have practised meditation regularly over time.[50] Given the potential for feeling threatened in your role, you need consciously to activate your own 'off switch' if you are to avoid the impact of constant stress on your mind and body.

Helpful habit #3: Consciously dial down your stress response by deep breathing

We have talked about the importance of practising awareness or mindfulness in order to receive the messages your body is giving you. Another aspect of this type of 'stilling' is the ability to observe your thoughts without getting caught up in them. When you engage in focusing on the present, you will have found that your mind intrudes with thoughts of the past, or with anticipation of the future.

---

50   Goleman, D. (1988): *Working with Emotional Intelligence*. London: Bloomsbury.

In the exercise above you were encouraged gently to bring your attention back to the breath on those occasions. Another way of responding is to practise simply noticing the thoughts and letting them go. They become like clouds in the sky; one dark and threatening, and another white and fluffy. You do not have to try to follow them, just notice and let them go.

Many people take their work home with them, if not in a briefcase, then in their head. They find it difficult to switch off from work particularly if there are things they have not yet completed and are worried about forgetting. In his book *The Off Switch*, Mark Cropley shares the results of his research into the impact of mentally taking work home.[51] His work suggests that those who are able to switch off and unwind at the end of the working day are not only healthier and happier, but also more productive. Studying data on mental health collected by the Office for National Statistics he categorised respondents to the survey into either 'high ruminators', those who find it difficult to switch off, or 'low ruminators', who do not. High ruminators are people who mentally 'chew over' the events of work, whether in retrospect or anticipation.

51   Cropley, M. (2015): *The Off Switch*. London: Virgin Books.

The study revealed that high ruminators were around 4.5 times more likely to report irritability and fatigue than low ruminators, and 3.5 times more likely to report sleep problems. They were 6.5 times more likely to report concentration problems. Professor Cropley recognises teaching as a stressful occupation.

In one of the studies reported in the book, he sampled a group of 108 schoolteachers, testing their cortisol levels first thing in the morning and at night. (Cortisol, you will remember, is elevated in the body's threat response). The natural pattern is for cortisol levels in the body to peak about 30-45 minutes after waking and gradually decline during the day until its lowest point at about 10pm, which signals a need for sleep. At the same time the natural rhythm of melatonin secretion (helpful in ensuring refreshing sleep) works in inverse proportion to that of cortisol: it is higher in the evening when it is time for sleep. The cortisol readings were tied to teachers' self-reports concerning how much they had thought about work. Those who reported high rumination showed significantly greater cortisol secretion in the evening, and lower early morning cortisol when compared to the low ruminators. Remembering that prolonged elevated cortisol levels have been linked to damage to the immune system, increased abdominal fat, inability to concentrate and so on, it is in your interest and that of your organisation that you become good at switching off.

Very often rumination is driven by an emotional concern: we fear we will not meet a particular deadline, or our inability to resolve a difficulty causes us to feel inadequate. Our response to external factors is influenced by the stories we tell ourselves. Sometimes our expectations are unrealistic. When working with clergy clients I have occasionally found myself saying: 'you and I are not going to change the Church of England between us.' A school leader talking about the difficulty of letting go of child protection issues described how she had learned to compartmentalise these issues and leave them at school. She had recognised that there was a limit to how much she could do. When we are able to observe our thoughts without becoming entangled and entrapped by them, we are more able to switch off from work at the end of the day.

Helpful habit #4: Establish boundaries – learn to distinguish between those things you can change from those you cannot and let the latter go

Cropley identifies two different approaches to taking work home: one is described above, and is not desirable for health. The second applies to you if you are someone who switches off work in the foreground of the mind. In doing so, you allow the unconscious to work on a problem, to which a solution will present itself as a sudden brainwave when you are putting the children to bed, preparing tomorrow's lunch, or brushing your teeth before bed. This is similar to the unconscious working overnight, when a solution to something you have been struggling with the previous day presents itself first thing in the morning.

Changing your mind

If you are a serial ruminator, changing this habit of a lifetime will not be easy, but it is possible. Just as you can change your emotional response to someone else by telling yourself a story about them that prompts a different emotional response, so telling yourself a different story about yourself can help you to break the habit of negative rumination. We will explore this in depth in the next chapter. In the meantime, if you are **aware** of your habit of ruminating, can **accept** that it would be beneficial to change and are prepared to take **action** to change your mind, you are three-quarters of the way towards establishing a new more helpful habit of thinking.

If you are a high ruminator, there are some physical activities you can engage in that may help you to switch off. One is to establish a routine that signals the end of the work day. I recall working with a headteacher once who consciously paused to 'say goodbye' to school at the end of the day, walking backwards for a few steps as he neared his car, placing his hands in front of him as though against a wall, which, in his imagination, now separated him from the preoccupations of school. Cropley's study reveals that those whose evening routine involves taking time to cook a meal in the evening – as opposed to quickly putting a ready-meal into the microwave – were more able to switch off, as were those who established a routine trip to the gym, a run, or something similar. Most of us have a work 'uniform', even if it is not the same as everyone else's. Even changing your clothes when you get home from work to signal to your body that you are now in a different environment, can make a difference.

When you start to establish new habits you need to make it easy for yourself. Notice your current routine, and where you might interrupt it. In the language of behavioural economics, consider how you might change your choice architecture. For example, if you habitually hang your coat on the same hook when you come in the door, put the clothes you are going to change into on the same hook, so that you have to move them to hang up your coat. If you habitually buy ready meals for each work evening, buy one less and cook instead. Look to increase the frequency of these changes over time, but avoid expecting too much all at once and setting yourself up to fail. If there is someone who would remind you of your resolution, ask them to do so. Research shows that declaring an intention publicly leads to an increased chance of success. Even better, make a pact with someone else who wants to change their habit, and support each other by reminding and congratulating each other when you achieve your goal.

The mind-body link

As we practise mindfulness, we become more aware of our physical sensations. What we may not be aware of is how we can take control of our physical state in order to have an impact on our mind. Some of this is about environment: it is hard to feel positive in dreary surroundings and, for example, hearing cheerful music can lift our spirits. We are used to the idea of body language being a means of non-verbal communication. We encourage others with a smile. We talk about 'open body language' being important in interviews; one way to help yourself to feel more confident is to sit or stand straight and raise your chin slightly. We know it is hard to feel depressed when smiling.

Amy Cuddy's book *Presence* takes a more scientific approach to the idea that we can affect how we feel by how we arrange our bodies.[52] If we are to engage our autonomy and change things, we need to exert power. As with everything else, our perception of our own power is affected by the stories we tell ourselves. One of the ways we communicate with our minds is through our bodies. If our bodies tell us we are powerful, we are more likely to feel powerful, and more able to take hold of our agency for change. In a series of experiments, Cuddy invited volunteers to adopt particular poses (without calling them 'high' or 'low' power) for two

---

52   Cuddy, A. (2015): *Presence*. London: Orion.

minutes to see whether there was any impact on hormonal secretion. Cuddy's claim that changes in body language had a direct effect on hormonal secretion of testosterone and cortisol has been questioned by researchers[53] who were unable to replicate the results. Significantly, her later work[54] refers to 'postural feedback' without mentioning hormonal changes. What is clear from her work, and that of others before her, is that subjective feelings of power influence both our thoughts and our behaviour. When we take control of our posture (deliberately standing tall, for example) we have a greater sense of power.

Helpful habit #5: change your body to change your mind

We should not confuse the simplicity of the notion of changing our bodies to change our minds with the challenge of action and adherence. Our thoughts and feelings come from a place deep within us: our core beliefs and values. They are a product of our life experience, the stories we have been told, those we have told ourselves, and the survival strategies we unconsciously choose in order to make sense of our experience and make our way in the world. We need to know more about these strategies and the truth of the stories before we can make a choice concerning whether we wish to continue to believe them, or risk letting go and finding our true shape.

Worth remembering

- If we want to change our habits to increase our energy, we need to take control of our minds and our bodies.
- What happens in our mind affects our body and vice versa.
- The first step to taking control is to be aware of our default behaviour.
- Developing new habits takes time and effort, but once established, it is cost free.
- We are more able to take control when we feel powerful. Checking and adjusting our body language can help us to feel more capable of change.

---

53 Simmons, J. P. & Simonsohn, U. (2017): Power posing: P-curving the evidence. *Psychological Science*, 28, pp. 687-693.

54 Cuddy, A., Schultz, J. & Fosse, N. (2018): P-Curving a More Comprehensive Body of Research on Postural Feedback Reveals Clear Evidential Value for Power-Posing Effects: Reply to Simmons and Simonsohn. *Psychological Science*, 29(4), pp. 656-666.

Chapter Five:
Core Beliefs and Values

The sun is shining through window of the children's playroom. Particles of dust dance in the sunlight, defying attempts to contain them. The sky outside has been rinsed early-morning blue, washed by the overnight summer rain. My two-year-old granddaughter is taking advantage of the habitual indulgence of grandparenthood to persuade me to read – again – one of her favourite books. As she climbs on to my lap to hear the story for the third time, I experience the glow of warmth that surrounds us all when we know we are truly loved. Upstairs her mother takes advantage of my presence to tidy up without the distraction of her daughter's 'help'. I can hear her footsteps overhead. As I pause in my reading of the story, I am aware of my granddaughter's body stiffening. She is suddenly alert and obviously disturbed. She jams her thumb into her mouth and curls herself tightly into my arms. I try to reassure her, 'it's only Mummy walking about upstairs.' Suddenly, I am taken back 60 years or so to my own childhood, and the fear of the sound of footsteps that emboldened me to cross the highway of ghosts, which was the corridor that separated the children's bedroom from that of our parents. What happened to that child, and where is she now?

It is known as a philosopher's conundrum, famously recorded by Plutarch in the first century, while writing the life of Theseus. Theseus ensured his ship was seaworthy by constantly replacing the parts that were damaged or rotten. Ultimately, he was forced to consider whether – with every plank replaced – it was in fact still the same ship. As we grow, many of the cells in our body are renewed over time; some die and are not replaced. We know this happens, but it has little impact on how we behave. What we are less conscious of as adults are the 'planks' that sustained and made us 'seaworthy' as children, which may now profitably be replaced. What happens to the children we once were? Part of my role as a coach is to enable individuals to explore their wants and needs. Change can feel threatening to our sense of self. If I change this aspect of my behaviour, will I be a different person? What will I lose about myself that I currently value? If sustaining resilience involves changing habits of behaviour and thought, do I have to become someone different to sustain resilience? Am I up for that? What will it cost? Each of us must answer those questions for ourselves. It can take us into deep territory, beyond the body and mind and into soul or spirit, touching our core beliefs and deeply held values.

In his 1943 paper *A Theory of Human Motivation*,[55] Abraham Maslow identified a theory of motivation driven by our needs. At its most basic, the primary human motivation amongst those who are mentally healthy is to survive. So we need food and water, shelter from extremes of weather and so on. Once we have those, we can think about what next. Beyond our physiological needs, come our psychological needs: to feel safe, to experience love, and feel worthwhile. These are 'deficiency needs'. They are conspicuous only by their absence. Once those needs are satisfied, goes the theory, we are in a position to work towards our higher needs: self-actualisation and self-transcendence. Of self-actualising people, Maslow says they are those who 'listen to their own voices, take responsibility, are honest ... they are involved in a cause outside of themselves'.

Hearing your own voice

Leaders will often tell you that they have changed since their first leadership role. Such change happens gradually, and is evident only with hindsight. At any time, they may strain to distinguish their own voice amidst the clamour and noise of others' expectations, the expectations

---

55 Maslow, A. (1965): Self-Actualization and Beyond. *Proceedings of the Conference on the Training of Counselors odf Adults* (pp. 108-131). Available at: http://files.eric.ed.gov/fulltext/ED012056.pdf [Accessed 26 October 2017].

of the system in which they operate, and their own expectations of themselves that they have never stopped to question. Our ability to distinguish our own voice allows us to make a conscious choice concerning which of those habits of thinking and behaviour that we have absorbed from others, we wish to adopt or maintain for ourselves. Without that discernment we may unwittingly continue to follow someone else's agenda. We follow a routine: clothing ourselves in the apparel that keeps us psychologically safe. We do so without thinking, or even knowing, that we might benefit from dressing differently – until the day when something causes us to question what we are wearing. We find ourselves questioning our life: 'is this it?', 'is this all there is?', 'who am I?', 'who do I want to be?', or even 'what about me?'.

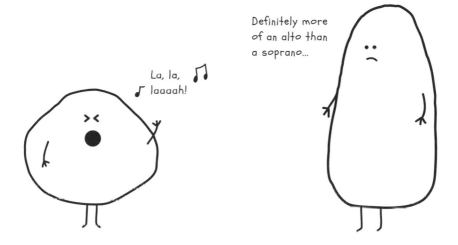

These are all manifestations of what Boyatzis calls 'the first discontinuity': the moment when you stop and consider your own journey through life, however you define that.[56] I have had the privilege of working with many individuals on their leadership journey. In a national training programme for future headteachers in the UK, one of the questions school leaders were encouraged to consider was: 'what sort of leader do

---

56   Boyatzis, R. E. (2006): An overview of intentional change from a complexity perspective. *Journal of Management Development*, 26 (7), 607-623.

you want to be?' They compared the leader they wished to be with the current reality, and formulated a plan to build on their strengths and address their development needs. They followed the steps identified by Boyatzis in creating **intentional** change, starting with the question: 'who am I as a leader?' The impetus for self-directed change is typically preceded by a pause, a taking-stock, often prompted by something external (in this case, the demands of a leadership programme) which demands that we look ahead and ask where we want to be in the future. Being a truly effective leader demands deep self-knowledge that enables us to understand the vulnerabilities and motivations hidden behind unconscious defences, which are established so early in life that we are unable to recognise them. Unless we consciously prioritise the self-exploration that leads us to greater understanding of what makes us who we are, and to what extent we wish to continue along the same track, our defences remain hidden and it is likely that undue stress will trigger a reaction, which we neither intend nor understand.

Most of us continue our journey through life without stopping to question whether we are taking the right path, until something happens to cause what Boyatzis refers to as the second discontinuity and to question 'am I a boiling frog?' – that is to say, am I allowing the pressures and priorities of daily life to take me in a direction which I have not chosen? Often it takes a significant critical life event to make us pause and reflect on how we live our lives and how that measures up to what we really want for the future. The untimely death of a friend, for example, will prompt us to realise how brief life is, and question whether we are living it to the full. The breakdown of a marriage, a period of mental or physical ill-health, rites of passage within our own family – such as a the birth of a child or grandchild, or a daughter or son leaving home for the first time – any of these may prompt us to ask the 'boiling frog' question. We have a great capacity for ignoring inconvenient truths; when we are in the midst of the chaos of everyday life, it is safer not to ask the big questions.

I have referred several times to Warren Bennis's assertion that leadership is a metaphor for centeredness, congruity and balance in one's life.[57] The Oxford English Dictionary's definition of the centre of gravity is as

---

57   Bennis, W. & Goldsmith, J. (1997): *Learning to Lead*. London: Nicholas Brealey.

follows: 'the central point in an object, about which its mass is evenly balanced'.[58] If you support your centre of gravity then you can remain in equilibrium in any position. You will be centred and remain balanced.

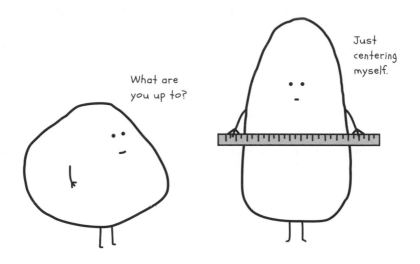

There are echoes of emotional resilience: 'the ability to remain on course and sustain emotional connection without being overwhelmed.' Strong emotional resilience allows us to remain balanced. On the tightrope of life, we may teeter on the brink of falling when things get really tough; an awareness of our centre of gravity will help us to regain our equilibrium. Congruity – the match between our inner selves and our outer expression of ourselves – also contributes. If the voice inside your head is telling you one thing and your external behaviour is displaying another, the opposing forces, at the very least, will lead you to struggle to maintain your balance. At worst, you will find yourself falling from the tightrope. Whose voices do you hear and how do you distinguish your own? What are the expectations of others that were given to you as a child, and will you be the same person if you abandon them? You cannot

---

58　Oxford University Press. (2012): *Paperback Oxford English Dictionary 7th Edition*. Oxford: Oxford University Press.

be completely congruent as a leader and as a human being, if you cannot hear your own voice.

In this penultimate chapter, we go beyond considering resilience in leadership, to consider what supports resilience in life. In the previous chapter we explored the amount of self-management that leadership calls for, and the degree to which such behaviour consumes energy. Congruent leadership allows its practitioner to accept and acknowledge his or her feelings; to identify the vulnerable self and the defences that keep it hidden. Such self-knowledge is the basis for growth. Many people with whom I have shared the emotional resilience model at the beginning of this book have nodded wisely, agreeing that it is in our interests to look after our own wellbeing as the first step to sustaining resilience. And yet they do not practise the behaviour that would lead them to establish such a habit. Many of us do not recognise our own needs. We prefer to believe that we are above average in capacity to continue to perform at our best without looking after our selves. Breakdowns, stress and disease happen to other people, but not to us.

Developing and sustaining resilience requires intentional change of habits of thinking and behaviour. If you have come this far with me on the journey, you will know that in order to develop new habits you need a sense of agency. That means stopping and taking control. A feeling of being out of control in a situation where you want to be in control leads to stress. If you are not able to control your own responses to external factors, you will not be able to sustain your resilience.

My personal and professional experience has taught me that our capacity for personal change exists in inverse relationship to our own fear. Those who work in schools are often driven by a need to care for others. Not infrequently, they find themselves so busy caring for others that they neglect their own needs. 'It's who I am,' they say, 'how can I care less?' No wonder we fear change if we confuse our behaviour with our being. Our behaviour is what we do; our being is who we are.

Like the ship of Theseus, over time, we change. Almost by default, our resilience increases as we learn that we can cope with the challenges life throws at us. Our preoccupations change. James Hollis talks about finding meaning in the second half of life.[59] He argues that our early adulthood is driven by the need to find a mate and procreate, and rests upon our childhood experiences that provide an unconscious pattern for our adult experiences. As a young mother, I remember feeling that the needs of my children and husband had eclipsed my own. I did not have the time or the space to question what my needs were or how I might meet them, but I do remember feeding my new baby in the silence of the night, and imagining that my life was being sucked from me in order to sustain his. Hollis suggests that our ego – our sense of worth – is too fragile to be deconstructed in the first half of life. Nature ensures that we do not have time to ask the question: 'who am I?' We talk about mid-life crisis and empty-nest syndrome as signifying stages of life that cause us to stop and ask these questions.

Wherever you are in your leadership journey, it is important not to wait for these moments before stopping to consider who you are as a leader and what drives your behaviour. You can do this alone, but if it provides an impetus for change, bear in mind that at the centre of Boytazis's intentional change model is resonant – sometimes interpreted as 'supportive' – relationships.[60] We owe to the late Nelson Mandela and Archbishop Desmond Tutu the widespread understanding of the South African concept of Ubuntu as 'a person is a person through other people'. We may think we know who we are, but we can test our position in the world only through interaction with others. We cannot grow and develop without other people to reflect back to us who we are. Growth is conditional upon the circumstances in which a living organism is placed. I have only to look on my kitchen windowsill to verify that nothing grows unless it has the right conditions to do so.

If, like many of my clients, you perceive your sense of self as bound to your habitual behaviour, you may well feel daunted by the prospect of examining deeply what drives your behaviour. Our behaviour is driven by our thoughts. Greater understanding of our thoughts allows us to develop a stronger sense of agency: when we take control of our thoughts and beliefs then we being to gain the capacity to make conscious choices concerning our own behaviour.

59   Hollis, J. (2005). *Finding Meaning in the Second Half of Life*. New York: Gotham Books.
60   Boyatzis, R. E. (2006): An overview of intentional change from a complexity perspective. *Journal of Management Development*, 26 (7), 607-623.

What drives our behaviour?

There are many ways of codifying behaviour. The Myers Briggs Type Indicator (MBTI) is, possibly, best known in business circles. It identifies 16 different combinations of preferences regarding how we interact with the world. Though frequently labelled as 'personality types', MBTI preferences indicate **preferred** behaviour. It is fairly straightforward to understand that if I prefer strawberries to raspberries, when both are available, I will choose strawberries. It does not mean that I will never eat raspberries. As we noted in chapter four, consciously choosing our behaviour, rather than responding instinctively, consumes energy. If you already know your MBTI type, you will have an insight into your preferred way of operating. Only licensed practitioners may use the full MBTI diagnostic, but there are many less well-researched versions freely available on the internet. Recognising our default behaviour and whether it helps or hinders in any particular situation allows us to choose to respond differently in order to achieve an outcome that is different from the one we are used to.

The humanist school of counselling and psychotherapy suggests that we grow up surrounded by conditions of worth. As children we learn that some of our behaviour is unacceptable. My sister apparently spat at the teapot when she was about two years old. She was having tea with my mother at someone else's house. As a relatively new parent, my mother was mortified, no doubt feeling that her daughter's behaviour reflected negatively on her parenting skills. I am quite sure that my sister would have been made very aware that this behaviour was unacceptable. We absorb more subtle messages during our childhood. As very young children we rely on the significant adults in our life for our survival; instinctively, we learn to manage our behaviour in order to ensure that our needs are met.

Every family system has its own set of rules, spoken and unspoken. Anger, for example, is a very natural emotion. If we were brought up in an environment where anger was not expressed, we learned not to show our anger. The image we project is of someone calm who does not get angry. When we feel anger, we cannot express it, for that would make us unacceptable to those who matter, so we hide it. The unexpressed anger becomes part of our negative self-image: we judge ourselves harshly because we 'know' that anger is unacceptable and yet that is what we feel. We imagine that if people knew we felt angry, they would think less of us. We are determined to hide it to avoid rejection, so the image we project to the world hides those aspects of ourselves that we find unacceptable. We learn to value the behaviour that was valued in our family of origin, or we may rebel against it. One way or another, whether through compliance or rebellion, the behaviour that was modelled to us and the behaviour that was rewarded or condemned, has an impact on the way we behave as adults.

Eric Berne's theories of transactional analysis tell us that seeking praise from significant adults in our life and avoiding injunctions leads us to behave in predictable ways.[61] We respond to similar situations in the same way, as though we have a script to follow. In the days of 21st century technology we might equally describe this behaviour as being like a computer programme. Push this button, and I will respond in this way; always the same way – until I am able to learn the code and re-programme the computer.

Building on the work of Eric Berne, Taibi Kahler identified five traits, or drivers of behaviour, and their characteristics.

---

61   Berne, E. (1961): *Transactional Analysis in Psychotherapy*. New York: Grove Press.

Table 1: Traits as drivers of behaviour

Trait	Characteristics
Be perfect	I produce reliable accurate work; I pay attention to detail and my work looks good. I'm well organised; I look ahead and plan how to deal with potential problems; it's important to me that projects run smoothly and efficiently. *Subtext: don't get things wrong.*
Please people	Maintaining friendly relationships is very important to me; I enjoy being with others and show genuine interest in them; I am concerned about others' feelings and will encourage them; I try to please others and sometimes do what I think they want without checking. *Subtext: avoid conflict and upset.*
Hurry up	I respond well to short deadlines and I'm motivated by pressure; I am excited and energised by having too much to do. I sometimes delay starting jobs until they become urgent; I am quick thinking and want to get on with things. *Subtext: it is not okay to be still; your value lies in what you achieve.*
Be strong	I stay calm under pressure and am energised by 'coping'. I can make difficult decisions about people without torturing myself about their impact; I can remain objective; I have a strong sense of duty. *Subtext: it is not okay to show emotion.*
Try hard	I tackle things enthusiastically and get most energy from having something new to do; given a project, I'll identify a whole range of ramifications and possibilities and will pick on things others may overlook. *Subtext: it does not matter whether you succeed, as long as you do your best.*

You may feel that you display all of these behaviours, and all of them are valuable in the right context. The test comes when you find you are unable to display these behaviours. Reflect on each of them in turn, and imagine how it is to display the opposite behaviour. How do you feel about yourself, for example, when you are caught out publicly making a mistake? Or when you have to give feedback to someone who you are pretty sure will take it badly? Or when you have nothing to do? What keeps you awake at night because you feel you have let down yourself or others? When we are under pressure our dominant traits come to the fore. If we know what they are, with practice, we can guard against their getting in the way of our intended outcomes and achievements.

Table 2: Traits and potentially unhelpful behaviour

Trait	Behaviour that may get in the way of what we are seeking to achieve
Be perfect	Difficult to regard something as finished; it can always be bettered. Minor changes at the last minute may delay things. I find it difficult to delegate because the others do not share my high standards. I may be perceived as over critical.
Please people	I may be reluctant to challenge, or confront issues, even when I know others are wrong. I may be reluctant to delegate for fear of overburdening others, with the result that I end up with too much to do. I find it difficult to say 'no' and may be perceived as lacking assertiveness.
Hurry up	I can seem intolerant or impatient when waiting for others who do not share my quick decision-making. I may interrupt others and/or finish their sentences to speed things up. I may misread others' communications and in haste, respond inappropriately.
Be strong	I see vulnerability as weakness and dislike acknowledging weaknesses. I may hide difficulties and take work home rather than ask for help; deep down I may be worried about asking for anything, lest it be refused.
Try hard	I tend to turn small projects into large ones, which makes them unmanageable for me and others. I love starting new things and don't always finish the old ones, or let others know that my priorities have changed, which can lead others to feel confused or frustrated.

Think back over scenes that you remember from your childhood. What were the mantras – those sayings that were often repeated? Some of those I have come across and the likely connection to the drivers of behaviour can include the following:

- Be perfect: 'if a job is worth doing, it is worth doing well' and 'appearances matter'.

- Please people: 'always put others first', 'be nice to each other, children' and 'do not argue'.

- Hurry up: 'the devil makes work for idle hands' and 'whistle and ride'.

- Be strong: 'big boys don't cry' and 'we always do our duty'.

- Try hard: 'always do your best' and 'if at first you don't succeed, try, try, try again'.

If you are struggling to identify your own drivers, ask someone who sees you in unguarded moments for their views. It is often easiest to spot when we are under pressure. When I have an overfilled diary and worry that I will not meet deadlines, I am inclined to half-read emails or rush to say 'yes' to an appointment without checking my diary properly, which results in further work. On these days, I have to remember to stop and take a breath, thus interrupting my default response.

In chapter one, I shared the story of my experience of being observed, when fear of failure took away my competence as a facilitator. Knowing my dominant traits allowed me to reflect on that experience after the event. My 'be perfect' told me that it was not okay to fail, especially when I felt compelled to justify the label of 'lead' facilitator. Of course, anyone who considers it is not okay to fail has a choice between getting involved in something new only if they are confident they cannot fail (and how would anyone do that?) or constantly telling themselves that they are not good enough.

I have caught myself engaged in both types of behaviour over the years. I have often taken on something new because someone else thought I could do it, rather than because I felt had the necessary skills. While I may have made a success of such endeavours, I have frequently felt that I am on the edge of the precipice of my own competence. If you have ever walked on a narrow footpath with the terrain sloping steeply down below you then you may be able to imagine how much fear I lived with on those occasions. We need to hold in mind that far from alienating us from others, it is our vulnerability and capacity for failure that connect us to the rest of humanity. If we are able to take account of the work of Kristin Neff who declares that she is a self-compassion evangelist, we may be able to learn self-compassion that in turn leads us to have greater compassion for others.[62]

I am sitting at my desk, dealing with emails, with one eye on the digital time display, conscious of the conference call I am expecting at 11am. I haven't worked with these people or this system before and I'm aware of feeling mildly anxious, hoping that the technology works and that the meeting goes well. Conference calls can be difficult. People talk over each other and it may not be immediately apparent who is talking unless they have a distinctive voice or say their name before every comment, or there is silence with everyone waiting for someone else to speak first. All these thoughts are in the back of my mind and, if I'm honest, I want to make a good impression. I have connected my mobile phone to its earpiece. I find this a more satisfactory way to converse, rather than jamming the phone against my ear.

It's 10:57am ... what can I do that takes three minutes? Then it occurs to me: I could just 'be'. I could not fill every minute with 60 seconds worth of distance run, as I was taught to do as a child. I could view time differently, acknowledging the value of mindfulness that I so often espouse to others and profess to be committed to. So I wait. I take a deep breath, close my eyes and focus on the sensations in my body. I am aware of a battle: one part says 'do something', while the other is saying 'wait', and I am reminded of the Goethe poem I learned for A Level German 'Warte nur, balde Ruhest du auch'. At 11am precisely the phone goes and I am greeted by an electronic voice that informs me that the meeting will start when the leader arrives. Music plays. Two minutes, then three, elapse; I am beginning to feel uneasy. What if I did something wrong in the registration and the meeting is going ahead without me? Will they think I haven't bothered to turn up? The seconds tick by and I am drumming my fingers

---

62   Neff, K. (2011): *Self Compassion*. New York: HarperCollins.

on the desk. The music stops. I hold my breath. Then it starts again. At five minutes, I email a colleague: 'I'm enjoying listening to the music. Is anything happening?' No reply. Perhaps she's already on the call ... Now I am really at the mercy of my hurry-up driver. I hit 'compose' on my email system, ready to email another colleague who will be on the call. The music stops and this time, the leader announces himself.

Even after two years of – inconsistent, it has to be acknowledged – mindfulness practice, the script I was given as a child is still a powerful driver of my behaviour. We need to separate our drivers of behaviour from their source in order to act in our own best interests.

Gremlins

Almost everyone will recognise that being unable to meet the demands of our habitual drivers of behaviour results in an inner conversation with our gremlin. It is that voice inside our head that tells us we are not enough: we are not clever enough, or kind enough, or quick enough, or strong enough, or capable enough. It sits on our shoulder, especially when we are tired, and criticises us. Our gremlins will upbraid us when we do not meet our own expectations and, worse still, they prevent us from putting ourselves in a situation that might expose us for the failure we feel ourselves to be. Its language is one of 'oughts' and 'shoulds' and its purpose is to keep us wedded to the rules and regulations by which we unconsciously live our lives. The 'oughts' and 'shoulds' may lead us in to difficulties, prompting us to act out of duty rather than love. Each of us needs to learn to respond to our gremlin in the way that works for us.

Minimising your gremlin's influence

The first step to minimising your gremlin's influence is to notice its voice. It has lived with you for such a long time that it has become hard to distinguish its voice from your own. It commonly has its roots in such underlying beliefs as:

- I am not lovable.
- I am a failure.
- Others are out to get me.
- I cannot act without the approval of others.

Such beliefs deter us from setting out on a road where we might come face to face with the real manifestation of our worst fears. As long as we do not put ourselves in a place where our fears might become a reality, we keep ourselves safe. Typical comments by our gremlin might be:

- You always get this wrong.
- You know you are not good at this.
- Who do you think you are?
- You are going to fall flat on your face.
- You will never make a success of it.
- It's safer not to be seen.

Remember the gremlin:

- is always fearful.
- wants to preserve the status quo.
- wants to keep you safe by holding you back.
- is not logical and you cannot reason with it.

Exercise 8: Minimising your gremlin's influence

1. Recognise it for what it is; notice when it speaks to you.
2. Give it a voice, face or shape, anything that allows you to crystallise it into something more concrete that an uneasy feeling that you can't engage with.
3. Imagine the embodiment of your gremlin were in the room and how would you challenge it?
4. Do anything you need to do to undermine it's credibility and impact (e.g. laugh at it, give it a silly name, shout at it, treat it with contempt).
5. The gremlin is always fearful; gently encourage and nurture it, as you would a fearful child.
6. Keep practising your strategy. Express it aloud and with conviction.

Yoo hoo. Guess who?!
Just here to remind you
that you're probably going
to mess this up. Again.
Until next time, toodle pip!

You might find that you recognise the voice as that of an individual in your past; it could be a teacher who told you at school that you would 'never make anything of yourself', or a parent who asked in despair, 'why must you always be so difficult?' It nags away at you when something has gone wrong, leading you to ruminate on your behaviour when you 'let yourself down' in other words, when you behave in a way that challenges your self-image.

I checked my mobile phone as I left the dentist that Monday morning. There was a message from the new headteacher of the school where I was Chair of Governors. 'We've had the call'. He did not need to explain: he meant that a visit from the schools' inspection service, Ofsted, would happen the following day. A further conversation highlighted the team's hypothesis: that governors had not challenged on standards. I spent the evening before the team arrived checking through the minutes of meetings annotating with post-it notes to make it easy for the team to find evidence of the governors challenging the school leadership, feeling grateful that I had done sufficient assessments in my time to know how important it is to make it easy for assessors to find the evidence that you want them to see.

Mid-morning on day one of the inspection, I had a call from the head. 'They're talking about failing the school because of inadequacies in our safeguarding arrangements' came the slightly breathless tone from the headteacher. My stomach lurched and I let out an involuntary expletive. This I had not been prepared for. We had a safeguarding governor who had recently had a meeting with the new headteacher to go through the local authority audit and check that things were in order. What Ofsted exposed was that, while we could put our hands on our hearts and say that certain training had taken place, the records took a considerable time to unearth, or were absent. Additionally, our policy had not been ratified for the new academic year, and still had the previous headteacher's name buried in the text. As Chair of the board, I had been metaphorically closing and locking the back door, blind to the fact that the front door and several of the windows were wide open.

And so it went on. The details of how we found ourselves discussing special measures with the lead inspector must remain confidential. Someone described it to me afterwards as 'a perfect storm'. It's true that a number of events had occurred simultaneously that left us more vulnerable than we realised at the time. If even one of those had not coincided with others, we might have been in a different place. The fact is that when I saw the evidence the team had pulled together, it was difficult to argue. As someone who is 'meant' to know about leadership, I was faced with the stark and unpalatable truth that the school had gone into special measures on my watch as Chair. My image of myself as someone who knows about leadership had been roundly and publicly challenged. I felt deep shame.

For many of us, our personal identity is closely intertwined with our work persona. I describe myself as a leadership development consultant, and yet here was I, leading an organisation that had been found wanting – and spectacularly so. In her TED talk 'Listening to Shame', Research Professor of Social Work at the University of Houston, Brené Brown, identifies the difference between shame and guilt. Guilt is when you think 'I did something bad'; shame comes from the feeling that 'I am something bad'. Shame paralyses us. It leads us to hide away. In my mind, everyone was identifying me as 'the person who thought she knew something about leadership, and then got found out'. (I have since discovered that – unsurprisingly – most people are far too preoccupied with their own journey to pay attention to mine, but I suspect one of the fantasies that shame creates is to consider that we are the focus of everyone's attention).

School leaders are often referred to as leading with 'moral purpose' and, if you check out the values identified on school websites, you will almost invariably find that schools profess themselves to be driven by such values as respect, responsibility, courage, perseverance, hope, and so on, all of which resonate with an organisation focused on developing future generations of responsible adults. If these values are to be lived throughout the school, we would expect that they would also be evident in the leaders' behaviour. It is possible, however, that a leader's determination to uphold these values can actually undermine his or her effectiveness. Let me explain.

In this context I describe 'values' as principles that guide our actions, and decisions in life. When our professed values are lived in practice, we are:

- conscious of them.
- aware of how they impact in our daily lives.
- aware of discomfort when they are compromised.

Richard Barrett aligns our values with our needs.[63] He says that our values reflect our motivations, and our motivations reflect our needs. Barrett defines 'consciousness' as 'a state of awareness of self (thoughts, feelings, ideas) based on a set of beliefs and values through which reality is interpreted.'[64] Barrett identifies two states of self that are developed through life: the survival self and the soul self. The focus of the survival self aligns closely with Maslow's hierarchy of needs, which I previously referred to – we need to attend to our physiological needs (food, clothing, shelter) and psychological needs (feeling safe, loved and having value) in order to survive. Where Maslow talks about 'self-actualisation', Barrett talks about 'transformation'. Barrett identifies this level as the gateway to

---

63   Barrett, R. (1998): *Liberating the Corporate Soul*. Woburn, Mass: Butterworth Heinemann.

64   Barrett, R. (1998): *Liberating the Corporate Soul*. Woburn, Mass: Butterworth Heinemann.

the soul self: the self that looks beyond its own survival to consciousness of the long-term needs of humanity and the planet, focusing on the common good.

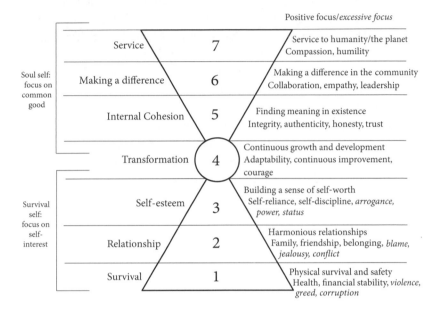

Figure 4: Seven levels of personal consciousness
Model © Barrett Values Centre® Adapted from training material with permission

Levels one to three here represent the survival-self, which may be driven by the fear of not having enough, or being enough. Levels five to seven, the soul self, are expressed when we let go of fear. We focus our attention on the lower levels in order to ensure our survival, often prompted by the voice of our gremlin. Only when we feel confident that our survival needs are met are we able to focus fully on the demands of the soul self, which yearns to make a positive difference to humanity and the planet. Fear undermines our ability to give our whole self – our agency. As we leave fear behind, we are able to focus our attention on the self-actualisation needs of the soul self.

The highest levels of 'making a difference' and 'service' are the natural territory of school leaders. The unique contribution of Barrett's model is to legitimise focus on the self, often ignored by school leaders in favour of focus on the school community. Leaders' unwillingness to acknowledge the importance of looking after themselves endangers the realisation of their vision: the very moral purpose they are striving to fulfil. Barrett suggests that we need to pay attention to all levels of consciousness; gaps in the lower levels may inhibit an individual's capacity to achieve at the higher levels. When our survival needs (physical and emotional) are not met, we unconsciously act out of fear. He suggests that the true test of how far we have progressed in our leadership journey is how we respond in the face of adversity: whether we 'descend into fear and react with I-based behaviours or pause, consider what's best for the common good and respond with understanding and compassion'.[65]

When I shared the seven levels model with a group of school leaders with whom I was discussing resilience, it was as though they suddenly saw the truth of the rhetoric that they had acknowledged but not acted on. They knew the 'oxygen mask' theory concerning taking care of oneself

---

65   Barrett, R. (2010): *The New Leadership Paradigm*. US and UK: The Values Centre.

in order to be able to give to others, but seeing the mapping of values in this way allowed them to recognise the interdependence of the lower and higher levels.

In the same way as our traits may lead us to undermine our intentions when we are under pressure, some of the values defined in levels one to three of Barrett's model may impact negatively on behaviour. In the diagram above you will see that levels one to three include behaviours that are the result of what is described as 'excessive focus'. No leader would be effective, for example, without the power to influence others, but an excessive focus on power is likely to be detrimental in its bid to take control of others and leave no room for others' views and approaches. On a personal level, most of us care what others think of us, but excessive focus on being liked could undermine our own integrity as we strive to be the person that others want or need us to be. Barrett argues that these values at the lower levels may be driven by fear. However safe, liked, or respected we are, our gremlins can convince us that it is not enough. You can map your values against the seven levels model by undertaking a free personal values assessment via the values centre website: www.valuescentre.com

Life is uncertain. If we did not take for granted that, generally, patterns are repeated, we probably could not live with the degree of anxiety we would feel. Most of us do not go to bed wondering whether the sun will rise in the morning. If we live in the UK, we know we are unlikely to be victims of a major earthquake, and so on. Our everyday survival needs are subtle and often hidden. Being left out of a group activity may threaten our sense of belonging, for example. When we fail we may question our own competence, imagining that we will lose the respect of others, or worse still, our job. These fears have an impact on our behaviour. When we perceive some sort of threat, says Barrett, we unconsciously act out of fear.

In his later work,[66] Barrett echoes James Hollis's argument, referred to earlier.[67] He aligns the seven levels of consciousness model with seven stages of psychological development. He views the lower stages as being

---

66   Barrett, R. (2017): *Stages of Psychological Development*. Available at: www.valuescentre.com/sites/default/files/uploads/The_Seven_Stages_of_Psychological_Development.pdf

67   Hollis, J. (2005): *Finding Meaning in the Second Half of Life*. New York: Gotham Books.

dedicated to the development of the ego, the upper levels as a stage of development when the ego and the needs of the soul are fully aligned. The latter is achieved when we have learned to access our own deeply held values through which we live a purpose-driven life, accessing our natural gifts and talents and following our calling.

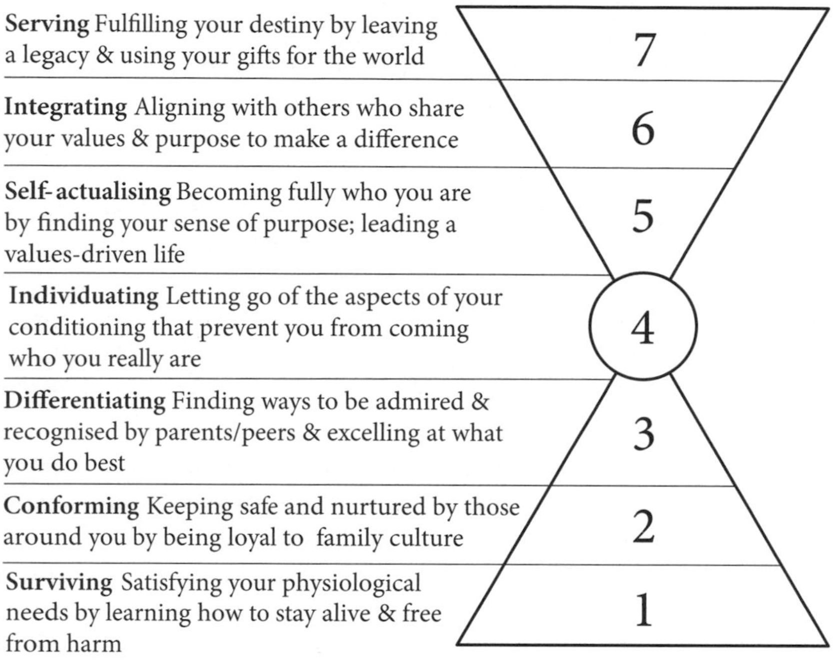

Serving Fulfilling your destiny by leaving a legacy & using your gifts for the world	7
Integrating Aligning with others who share your values & purpose to make a difference	6
Self-actualising Becoming fully who you are by finding your sense of purpose; leading a values-driven life	5
Individuating Letting go of the aspects of your conditioning that prevent you from coming who you really are	4
Differentiating Finding ways to be admired & recognised by parents/peers & excelling at what you do best	3
Conforming Keeping safe and nurtured by those around you by being loyal to family culture	2
Surviving Satisfying your physiological needs by learning how to stay alive & free from harm	1

Figure 5: Steven stages of psychological development
© Barrett Values Centre® Used with permission

Stage four of the seven stages of psychological development points to the need to let go of aspects of parental and cultural conditioning that are no longer useful; that prevent us from recognising our own voice, and thus inhibit our journey to know who we truly are, as people and as leaders.

I have worked with individuals on the threshold of headship who are reluctant to take that final step which leads to ultimate accountability for the school community. Often it is because they look at others in that position and say 'I could never do that' or 'I'm not good at …' whatever aspect of headship that they admire in another. It takes a while for them to understand that each of us has to find our own way of 'being' in leadership and in life. The ease with which we hear our own voice and achieve true authenticity depends both on our nature and nurture. By nurture I mean both our early influences, and the systems in which we now operate.

It is fear that keeps us locked in the lower levels of the Barrett model: fear that if we separate from our family system, we will be abandoned. Even rebellion is a form of connection to the system against which you are rebelling. The unchosen behaviour of our family is the invisible lifeline that keeps us connected to the mother ship. Without it we may fear drifting into space for a thousand years with no means of return. When we let go of the unchosen behaviour that gives us the illusion of safety, we act with a greater faith in our autonomy.

Most of us, consciously or unconsciously, live with a degree of fear. In order for the human race to survive as a species, the ego has to be strong enough to withstand the challenges of a fragile life. Although we know intellectually that we will all die, our ego prefers not to acknowledge the fact. Irv Yalom's *Staring at the Sun* suggests that – once we are able to stare at the sun: to bear the pain of gazing unblinking in to the face of our own death – other anxieties diminish.[68] From the earliest experiences of childhood, when we conformed to the expectations of our family and adopted their 'script', we learned to adapt our behaviour in order to feel safe. I do not wish to imply that our traits and drivers of behaviour are a negative force. When you reflected on the traits identified by Taibi Kahler above, you may have felt very positive about those that you recognise in yourself. You may want to thank your parents for inculcating that particular behaviour within you. The dark side of valuing such behaviour is the fears that arise when we do not meet our own expectations (which, of course, are actually others' expectations). The point here is that we may unconsciously act out of fear and discount our true feelings. We need to make friends with our fears and see them for what they are if we are to escape their hold on us.

---

68   Yalom, I. D. (2008): *Staring at the Sun*. San Francisco: Jossey-Bass.

From talking to my sons, I know that events that had a significant impact on them as children are often events of which I have no memory, and vice versa. Similarly, my parents have told me about events in my early life that I believe, but cannot recall. We live with family stories, knowing that memory is far from reliable. What is the earliest memory that you have which belongs to you alone? My earliest memory dates from when I was about three years old, which is commonly accepted as the earliest age at which memories are retained. Work by Dr Patricia Bauer of Emory University suggests that, in order to be able to store autobiographical memory, we have to have developed a sense of time and place, as well as developing a sense of self as a separate individual, with a perspective all of our own. Before the age of about three, our neurological architecture is insufficiently developed to allow us to encode memories in the same way as we do later in life.

So does that mean that, in place of memory, is a blank slate from nought to three years old? Something happened between birth and three years old, and, indeed, babies' experience in the womb affects their physical and neurological development. Can it be true that if we have no recall of events, they have no impact on us? As science advances, it becomes clear that whether we remember them or not, our earliest experiences do have an impact on who we are and how we behave. There is a body of knowledge that suggests that there are two types of memory.[69] The first may be described as explicit, or declarative memory, traditionally understood as that which allows us to place our memories in time and space. It allows us to distinguish between things that happened yesterday and things that happened years ago. The second is implicit memory, which is stored as memory in our body, and manifests itself in habits of behaviour; it allows us to remember things like how to walk. From pre-birth and into early childhood, neural pathways are developing with incredible speed. Connections are developing; our brains are being wired to understand the world in a particular way. The neural pathways developed early in life drive the habits of behaviour that remain with us into adulthood.

Whatever our starting point, whatever early experiences may have impacted on our habits, there is now considerable evidence of the brain's neuroplasticity – its capacity to change and develop over time. Before the days of satellite navigation, London taxi drivers were famously shown to have enlarged hippocampi, through the extraordinary development of their memory for the geography of London. In chapter two, we saw how meditation affects the activity of the amygdala, making it less inclined to heightened activity and quicker to recover than the amygdala of those who have not practised meditation. With practice, we can build new neural pathways, but this only occurs if we are conscious of the need to do so, and if we consciously focus on practising until we become unconsciously competent.

Carl Rogers, often described as the father of humanist person-centred psychology, proposed the notion that human beings have a need to develop and grow and are able to do so if the conditions are right. We are born with a strong sense of our own needs, which reside in the 'organismic' self, the self that trusts its own experience and has the potential to grow and flourish. As babies, we know our needs and our first demand is that they should be met. Our limited experience of life is unmediated by others' expectations: the only way others know our needs is through our crying. If we are lucky, someone responds to that crying and we feel comforted.

---

69   van der Kolk, B. (2014): *The Body Keeps the Score*. London: Allen Lane.

A hundred years ago, and even more recently, babies were parented differently. 'You'll make a rod for your own back if you keep attending to that child when it cries' was a warning given to new mothers by previous generations. 'On-demand' feeding taught babies that – despite what their bodies were telling them – it was not time to eat.

Imagine the baby 18 months or so later, and watch the toddler fall over and cry. A loving mother picks him up and tries to reassure him. 'It's alright, don't cry,' she says, 'you're not hurt'. Self-regulation, you will remember, is the role of the pre-frontal cortext (PFC). Babies' brains do not develop the capability of the pre-frontal cortex until they are about three years old. Before that, they are incapable of self-regulation, and rely on the emotional connection with parents or significant others to know what keeps them safe. The mother is teaching her child how to self-regulate, but at an emotional rather than a cognitive level. The child feels comforted in the mother's arms and learns that the warmth of her nurturing presence can ameliorate pain. In the early stages of life, it is in the child's interests to trust those who care for him.

This is the start of the journey that leads us to experience the conditions of worth referred to earlier in this chapter and results in the development of our conditional self: the self we love and accept when it behaves in a particular way. It leads us to mistrust our own authentic experience of life that significant others have discounted. As the child separates from the mother, his challenge is to develop a sense of himself as an individual who is separate from his mother, and to understand and experience what it means to be in intimate healthy relationship with another. This is the yin and yang of human life: to live in healthy relationship with another while retaining our own autonomy; to be able to make choices that avoid undue reliance on the good opinion of others (real or imagined), and to be comfortable with our own company, while not fearing the company of others or the perceived pressure of an intimate relationship.

The doctor's upstairs waiting room is quite small. Blue upright chairs stand with their backs against the walls. About a third of them are taken. To the right and left of me are vacant chairs. In the corner is a toy box that has my three-year-old son's attention. Occasional glances and smiles from others in the room encourage me to relax, as I wait to take him for his routine vaccination. Now it is our turn and I take his hand and enter the doctor's surgery. Everything is going smoothly until the doctor gets out the needle and asks me to hold on to him tightly. He screams and wriggles and it is quite impossible for the doctor to complete his task. We return to the waiting room for my son to calm down. He is crying hard now; I am feeling hot with the judgement of others, who I imagine are regarding me as an incapable parent, unable to get my child to comply with this simple requirement. Again we are called. I get halfway along the corridor with him this time, before he anticipates the end of the journey and starts crying loudly, dragging his heels so that I have to pick him up. Again we return to the waiting room. In my head the judgemental voices are now saying, 'what's the matter with her? Why doesn't she just give him a slap and tell him to do as he's told?' Slapping was not in my repertoire; bribing and pleading and encouraging were, but nothing seemed to be working, and I was feeling more and more anxious and incompetent.

Hearing the noise, the practice health visitor came to show me to another room where we talked while my son played on the toy cooker, distracted by his delight in the cooker-rings that showed red when he turned the switches on the front. Between us, we eventually persuaded him to have his injection. I still remember, with gratitude, the health visitor's comment to me 'He needs so much love,' she said with compassion, smiling, as she looked at his tear-stained face. I knew that she was right. Frightened and confused, he still needed to feel loved and accepted. He didn't need to feel that I loved him only when he did as he was told and didn't embarrass me in front of others. In that moment, the feelings of judgement by others (which were, of course, really my own conditions of worth judging me for not meeting the stereotypical requirements of a good parent whose child does as he is told) dispersed. The resident professional had verified my instincts: fear is best conquered by love.

I wish I could say that my sons had been surrounded by unconditional love as they grew; I know that is not true. The work of Franz Ruppert and others identifies the multi-generational impact of early experiences of trauma.[70] Much of what we experience in early childhood results from

---

70   Ruppert, F. (Ed.) (2016): *Early Trauma* (English Language Edition ed.). (J. Stuebs, Trans.) Steyning: Green Balloon Publishing.

the experiences of earlier generations. The definition of trauma here is different from the way we tend to use the word in everyday life. We often think of childhood trauma as the type of thing that parents are punished for: neglect, violent aggression, sexual, and physical abuse. Then there is the trauma caused by war or famine or earthquake or world disasters. Even if these happened to you before you were able to store them as explicit memory, it is likely that someone will have told you about these events; they are obvious sources of trauma.

Much more common – and generally unknown to the conscious mind – is the trauma that occurs when a being experiences a threat to its physical or emotional survival that is invisible to others. Whether there was a real chance of the event leading to extinction is not important: it is the perception of the threat to survival that matters. When the trauma becomes overwhelming and inescapable, it results in a split in the psyche.

Imagine a baby in the womb who experiences a feeling of high anxiety through his mother's nervous system, for example. If he could run away, he would, but he cannot. The threat becomes unbearable and the only way to escape is through dissociation: the psyche splits. The traumatised part splits off from the part that operates from a position of healthy autonomy – that is to say that part of ourselves that listens to and responds to the world from the truth of our own experience. The traumatised part is kept hidden by the survival part, whose sole ambition is to protect the psyche from the experiences and emotions of the trauma. The capacity of healthy autonomy is reduced. A great deal of unconscious energy is required to keep the trauma hidden, involving unconscious survival strategies. So now there are three parts of the psyche: the healthy part, the traumatised part, and the survival part. As we are unaware of our survival strategies, or our traumatised self, they compromise our capacity to choose to respond from a place of healthy autonomy.

This is more common than you might think, for the very reason that such trauma can be unwittingly passed down the generations. As psychologically healthy adults, we have the capacity to sustain intimate relationships, and to be separate and independent. Intimate relationships are about enjoyment and enrichment, not about survival. The first intimate relationship we experience is that with our mother, who carries us through gestation: she and I are one. At this stage, we depend totally on our mothers for survival, for food and comfort. The needs of the newborn infant are hardly less demanding, even though the child is now a separate organism. When the mother is physically or emotionally absent, possibly operating from her own survival strategies, she is unable to meet her infant's needs, causing the latter to look elsewhere. The instinct of the infant is to do all he can to get his needs met. If his survival needs are neglected, this will be experienced as life threatening, hence a trauma.

Additionally, the mother may be communicating her own feelings of trauma to the infant; after all, before birth, they are biologically connected. Anxiety felt by the mother is also felt by the infant, and for the infant, apparently safe in the womb, there is no escape. A threat with no means of escape is traumatic to the unborn child. A mother who has experienced unresolved trauma will be living in part through her survival strategies. She unwittingly passes on her feelings of trauma to her child, whose psyche splits to keep the feelings of trauma hidden; survival strategies develop instead, and the infant's capacity for healthy autonomy is diminished. And so it continues through the generations and through life, as survival strategies are triggered by fear of re-traumatisation.

When we lose our capacity for healthy autonomy, we find ourselves entangled with other people's agendas and survival strategies. The more entrenched the survival strategies, the more confused we become about what we really want: what is 'good for us'. Unconsciously we fear re-enactment of the trauma. We live with anxiety without necessarily being able to give it a name. Elsewhere I have referred to being 'pushed out of shape' by others' demands. When we are operating from a place of healthy autonomy, we are clear about our boundaries: where we end and where others begin. What we want for ourselves is no longer unconsciously compromised by what others demand of us. As we grow our healthy autonomy through integration of the split-off parts of ourselves, we become clearer about our boundaries and who we are, and do not rely on others to compensate for the parts of ourselves we find unacceptable. Having worked with a practitioner of Franz Ruppert's methods, I find myself more able to act from a position of healthy autonomy. It is a slow and sometimes difficult journey that requires courage and patience. If we have in our sights the desire to become a 'fully integrated human being', leading our own life from a place of healthy autonomy, it is a journey worth making with the support of an expert guide.

Some of the impact of my parenting on my sons is not clear to me; that is a journey of discovery they will need to make for themselves if they wish to, when the time is right. I have to regard my parenting as 'good enough' – a standard which I have become much more able to accept, acknowledging that perfection is unattainable – but I will certainly have passed on some of my insecurities. Self-examination and feedback can help us to understand our childhood 'scripts', and how they impact on our adult life. We begin to understand some of the baggage that others have given us, which we can choose to put down. What is harder to address, requiring a journey of deeper exploration, is the impact of our pre-verbal experiences on our development, or even those which happened pre-birth, of which we have no conscious memory. It is not easy, or possibly even advisable, to explore this area without the support of a specialist. Vivian Broughton's book, *Becoming Your True Self*, is a brief helpful introduction to the subject.[71] Beyond that, if it is something you wish to pursue, it is worth seeking a practitioner of Franz Ruppert's methods.

Worth remembering

- If we are to develop a true sense of our own agency, we have to be able to distinguish our own from others' voices.
- Becoming an 'integrated human being' requires us to become consciously competent in listening to and accepting ourselves.
- Fear can undermine our best intentions.
- We need to face, understand and accept our fears if they are not to prevent our acting from a place of healthy autonomy.

---

71   Broughton, V. (2014): *Becoming Your True Self*. Steyning: Green Balloon Publishing.

At birth, our most significant relationship is with our primary caregivers, but we are also part of the family system. As a second child (of two) I experienced no need to adapt to a new arrival: my big sister was always there. The moment I started school, I became part of another system, and that system operated as part of the education system. We are affected by and influence the systems in which we operate. We cannot leave the subject of emotional resilience for leadership in schools without considering the impact of the system on leaders who operate within it.

Chapter Six:
The Influence of the System

Without discussion, the group sort themselves into a circle, as though replicating a clock-face, with the longest-serving member of staff at 12pm; next to her the next longest-serving and so on. In some places, empty chairs represent colleagues who have come and gone. At about the figure 4 on the clock face, there is a large gap with no chairs.

'What's happening here?' I ask.

'Oh, that's the lump,' explains one member of the group, as though it's fairly obvious.

'The lump?' I question.

'Yes. That was an awful time, when the school failed its inspection. The head left and someone new came in.'

There follows an explanation of the shame felt by staff when they were told that the school was not good enough and was failing to provide for its children an acceptable standard of education. Ten years later, it is evident that some are still mourning the loss of the headteacher ('a lovely man') who left under a cloud, unacknowledged for the good things that had happened during his headship. A member of the group, who has previously been silent, suddenly seems to come alive as she shares stories of the school's involvement with the local community at that time, regretting that such events are no longer happening. It now becomes clear to me that the issues I have been brought in to address have their origins in events of an earlier time, precipitated by a system that sought to name and unceremoniously remove a single individual for failing to influence sufficiently the complex and unpredictable moving parts of its machine. Not for the first time, I wonder what it would take to build a system that combines compassion and accountability.

In the preceding pages, we have explored some of the factors that interact to influence our capacity for emotional resilience. We know that wellbeing enhances energy and we need to notice and take control of how we use our energy. When we understand how much of our energy is drained by unconscious habits that are no longer useful to us, we can make a decision concerning which habits of thinking and behaviour we want to retain and which it would be helpful to replace. We have considered the impact of our upbringing on who we have become and how much of who we are now is influenced by our early experiences and environment. When we reflect on our past experiences, we can begin to understand their significance in shaping the individuals we are today. It stands to reason, then, that today's experiences will have an impact on how we behave and who we become in the future. We have begun to gain an insight into the influence of the first system we encounter: our family system. There are many other systems that we are part of. In fact, we are all part of a complex inter-related web of many systems. A system may be defined as 'a collection of individual agents with freedom to act in ways that are not always totally predictable, and whose actions are interconnected so that one agent's actions changes the context for other agents'.[72]

When we understand our interactions as starting and ending solely with our one-to-one or one-to-many encounters, we miss a significant dimension of life's shaping forces. When we disregard the universal language of systems, it is a little like listening to a text message inadvertently sent to a landline, relayed by a robotic voice: it conveys each word separately but with no understanding of the overall message. Each of us influences, and is influenced by, the systems in which we operate. When you interact with your colleague, he or she is listening through the filters of his or her own family system and both of you are being influenced by the school

---

72   Plsek, P. E. & Greenhalgh, T. (2001): The challenge of complexity in health care. *BMJ Clinical Research*, 323 (7313), 625-628.

and wider education system in which you operate. When we ignore the influence of the system, we are likely to use the wrong tools to achieve what we want to achieve, and blame ourselves for being ineffective.

If thinking about systems rather than individuals is new to you, you might want to take a few moments to consider some of the systems that you influence, and are influenced by, in your daily life. In the previous chapter we highlighted the impact of our family system, but there are many more. Society itself is a system, influenced by the many systems that operate within it, such as the education system, the judicial system, the public sector system, the political system, and so on. All of us operate in the global eco-system. Not only are each of these systems influenced by internal changes to its constituent parts, each system also has the capacity to cause change in other systems, and every person operating in each system is influenced by their own systems.

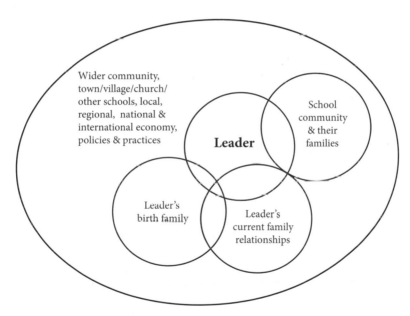

Figure 6: Overlapping influences of systems

'No man is an island' said the poet John Donne in the 17th century. Our world is made up of interconnected and interdependent systems. For each system that involves individual components, there is a separate system that belongs to that component, until we reach the nucleus of an atom. When the constituent parts of a system work together, the system has a creative energy of its own. When the constituent parts work against each other, the energy becomes destructive. It is evident in nations ripped apart by civil war, in dysfunctional teams and organisations, and in ecological systems, where the balance between the needs of humanity have disregarded the needs of the ecosystem. It is even evident within the human body, where stress impacts negatively on the immune system. Gabor Maté highlights the interconnectedness of biological systems.[73] He is critical of his own medical profession for its failure to look beyond physical symptoms when seeking a cause for ill-health, discounting the interconnectedness of body and mind. 'We have all but forgotten,' he says, 'that the terrain for illness is a particular human being at a particular time of his life history.' A straightforward 'cause and effect' model of disease disregards the interconnections of mind, body, and environment, which create ill-health. A straightforward cause and effect model applied to pupils' attainment disregards the interconnections and influences of the broader environment on pupils, teachers and schools.

The 2010 government white paper, *The Importance of Teaching*, heralded the drive to 'create a school system which is more effectively self-improving'[74] and with it the notion of system leadership. The strategy included providing greater freedoms for individual schools, decentralisation, and handing responsibility for improving education to the education professionals. It reduced the accountability of schools that were judged to be outstanding, by removing the need for such schools to be inspected in the usual inspection cycle. Stronger schools were charged with supporting those that were struggling, through the deployment of 'system leaders' – mostly headteachers who had a record of school improvement. Later there was an opportunity for leaders at other levels of the system to be designated as national, or specialist leaders. Outstanding schools became National Support Schools. There was an increased imperative – both stated and implicit – that all professionals should work together to address the challenges facing education.

---

73   Maté, G. (2003): *When the body says no.* Toronto: Random House.
74   Department for Education (DfE). (2010): *The Importance of Teaching.* London: HMSO.

Senge identifies systems thinking as needing the disciplines of 'building shared vision, mental models and personal mastery to realise its potential'.[75] Shared vision is necessary if we are to commit to long-term thinking; awareness of current mental models allow us to identify the flaws in our current ways of seeing the world; and personal mastery of systems thinking gives individuals the motivation and ability to learn how our actions affect our world. For learning to flourish, he suggests, it needs to take place in a no-blame culture. Echoing the arguments outlined by Barrett, he points to the need for the values that underpin the vision to go beyond meeting the needs of employees, customers and shareholders.[76] Successful organisations have a bigger vision: to contribute to the long-term future of the world.

Shared vision and values

School leadership is often described as being driven by moral purpose. Many of the school leaders I have worked with articulate their values clearly and demonstrate them in the way they behave. With some notable exceptions, however, few schools have a systematic way of measuring whether those who are part of their community experience their values. What about the school system as a whole? There are many different views concerning the purpose of education and an even greater variance concerning how to prioritise the different strands of school improvement. School leaders' values are likely to have a significant impact on the way their schools operate. Schools are also affected by the values experienced within the education system. What does it mean to value diversity in a town where a comprehensive school's intake is skewed by parents with the resources to make a choice concerning where to send their children to school? If the best way to improve a primary school's reputation is to raise standards of attainment, which will increase its popularity and ultimately provide greater resources and resourcefulness, is that a justification for spending months at a time on maths and English, in order to improve the school's attainment data while depriving pupils of a broader experience that might provide greater motivation to learn?

---

75   Senge, P. (1992): *The Fifth Discipline.* Toronto: Random House.
76   Barrett, R. (1998): *Liberating the Corporate Soul.* Woburn, Mass: Butterworth Heinemann.

Headteachers are faced with dilemmas that arise from a target-driven agenda. They are focused not only on learning, but also on standards, value for money and political agendas. Individual leaders may find their values are tested by the decisions that the system demands of them. Should they exclude a disruptive pupil from an unsupportive family, or put additional pressure on staff and the pupils? Should they comply with curriculum demands to the letter and risk alienating students by so doing? In the words of a primary headteacher: 'If I turn my attention to local or national government, I turn my back on the pupil.'[77]

These and other dilemmas faced by school leaders arise from the context in which they operate. Each dilemma demands a little more of their energy, as they try to marry their own values in the face of conflicting demands. Working across the system to help other schools might be seen as altruistic; it also comes at a cost. The arguments for economies of scale and greater flexibility in the use of resources will take us only so far. When resources are scarce, securing the future of your own school or trust is a necessary pre-requisite of supporting others. It is a small step from securing the future of your own school **before** supporting others to securing the future of your own school **through** supporting others; in other words taking on additional schools in order to bolster your own budget. School improvement then becomes a commercial operation, subject to free market principles, focused on profitability. Schools that are assessed as being a bad investment, whether economically or educationally, will be left behind. Systems-thinking demands a long-term perspective, says Senge, yet by definition, none of us is here long enough to learn from the long-term impact of our current decisions.

Long-term thinking

Senge highlights the dangers of taking a traditional linear view of cause and effect. 'When we act in a complex system the consequences of our actions are neither immediate nor unambiguous. Often, they are far removed from us in time and space.'[78] We need to consider the long-term effects of our actions, even though we may not be able to predict them.

---

77   Hammersley-Fletcher, L. (2013): Value(s)-Driven Decision Making. *Educational Management, Administration and Leadership*, 43 (2).

78   Senge, P. (1992): *The Fifth Discipline*. Toronto: Random House, p. 313.

A significant difficulty here is that education is political; politics and patience do not sit well together. Governments need to prove the efficacy of their policies quickly if they are to be re-elected. Rightly concerned with the economic prosperity of the nation, governments seek a system that guarantees children are literate, numerate and appropriately prepared for the next stage of their education. This, it is said, is the responsibility of the school system, discounting the role of the first educator of any child: that of the parent, carer or other parenting figure, and the place of the environment in nurturing any organism.

Just as Maté highlights the inadequacy of a straightforward 'cause and effect' model of disease, so we need to be wary of a straightforward cause and effect judgement about schools that are deemed to be failing. Senge alerts us to the danger of this approach leading to more pressures in the long term.[79] If we are to take account of systems thinking in our model of school improvement, we need to focus on a vision far beyond the term of a single government. If they are to resist the pressures of the system, leaders need to expand their understanding and influence, whilst also accepting the limits of their capacity.

The questions we ask about school improvement are apt to encourage us to look for cause to be close to effect and discount the wider system. When children are not making progress, we generally seek the cause in teaching; when teaching is not having the expected impact, we seek the cause in leadership; when leaders are not dealing with inadequate teaching, we seek the cause in poor governance. Rarely do we move outside the immediate terrain and ask what it is about the wider system that has contributed to the failure of education. As public funds are increasingly over-stretched, linear thinking that releases funds in the short term – such as increasing class sizes to reduce the number of teachers on the payroll – may have a negative impact in the long term. The potential impact on students' results and teachers' and students' wellbeing is hard to quantify in advance and may ultimately be too high a price to pay.

---

79   Segne, P. (2004): *The leader's new work: Building Learning organisations*. In K, Starkey, S, Tempest & A, McKinlay (eds). How organisations learn: Managing the search for knowledge (pp. 462-486). London: Thomson.

When a school is found wanting by the inspection system, the system responds – more often than not – by removing the leadership without honouring any of the good that has been achieved in the past. In our quest to make the best possible use of public funds, we sacrifice humanity on the altar of efficiency, arguing that we are focused on the common good and educating the next generation; so the end justifies the means. What we fail to notice is the stress that this approach generates within the wider system, and its impact on the very individuals on whom we rely for the long-term needs of the system.

We cannot change the past, but we can seek to understand its impact on the present. We know we are educating children for a future that does not yet exist, but we continue to operate a system that relies on models of the past, with schools stretching their resources to fill the gaps that were previously taken care of in the wider community. Schools are open for longer to compensate for parents and carers who are unable to be at home at the same time as their children; breakfast clubs provide a nutritious start to the day when it is difficult or impossible for that to be provided at home. In many homes, the economic necessity of those working to maintain the family, sometimes juggling several jobs, puts a significant strain on time and space to share with their children. Many of those working in schools are also parents or carers; when they are put under pressure, they inevitably take it home.

I have had several conversations with teachers and leaders who have adjusted their way of working when they realised that they were spending so much time concerned with other people's children, that they were finding little time for their own. The school system is charged with taking account of the wellbeing of staff and pupils, whilst apparently not noticing the part it plays in undermining the wellbeing of those who operate within it. My experience of working with groups of schools tells me that when we proactively build trust among and between institutions, learning benefits. Trust flies in the face of fear. If we were to adjust the system's models of accountability that encourage hiding our deficiencies to one where individuals and institutions feel safe enough to ask for help, future generations may benefit.

A no-blame culture

Every teacher knows that learning is undermined by a reluctance to be open about when things have gone awry, whether at the level of pupils' learning, or leaders' errors of judgement. The most effective learning organisations are underpinned by a no-blame culture. The concept of a 'self-improving system' relies on individuals within that system being open about their failures as well as their successes. My experience suggests the extent to which school leaders are prepared to share their failures and successes is – at least in part – related to a school's last Ofsted judgement and where it is in its regular cycle of school inspections. Just as you probably would not willingly decide to embark on building works on your house just before important guests arrive, leaders may be reluctant to try something new if they suspect an Ofsted inspection is imminent.

Despite the focus on the 'school system', accountability still rests with the individual. The role of the 'hero leader' in education was discredited long ago, yet there is still a demand within the system for a single individual to be held to account for the failure (in terms of what is measured) of an individual school. Balancing short- and long-term solutions is a challenge that faces every school leader. Several headteachers have spoken to me about what they regard as the 'football manager' approach: if your team fails, you lose your job. This approach sits unhappily alongside the no-blame learning culture for which Senge argues. A complete change in leadership may be an effective short-term strategy for an individual school. A significant long-term side effect is the impact on leaders themselves, highlighted in the opening of this book. The system invokes a fear of being found out, of being identified as 'not good enough' resulting in hyper-vigilance and uncertainty that evokes stress. When individuals feel under threat, they close down and it becomes increasingly difficult to ask for help. In Barrett's terms, they stop focusing on 'the common good' of their school, and focus instead on their survival needs.[80]

Leaders are still seen by the system as those who are expected to solve problems whose origins often lie far beyond their reach. It takes time to change the culture of an organisation; it takes generations to change the

---

80   Barrett, R. (1998): *Liberating the Corporate Soul*. Woburn, Mass: Butterworth Heinemann.

culture of a community. A school leader may be held accountable for the school's contribution to, and interaction with, the local community. To suggest that he or she is **responsible** for the community, however, infantilises the parents, staff, governors and members of support services that make up that community. Leaders, whose personal identity is heavily invested in the reputation of their schools, will find it difficult to accept that they are not responsible for many of the aspects of education for which they are held accountable. Their fear of failure adds to the stress in the system and, in some cases, their decision to leave.

Leaders within the education system face what Keith Grint refers to as a 'wicked problem'.[81] He argues that problems that have been encountered previously, which we know how to solve, are 'tame' problems. 'Wicked' problems, by definition, are more complex and require the input of the whole community. Wicked problems require transfer of authority from the individual leader to the collective, in an attempt to come to terms with the problem. The role of the leader is not to solve the problem in this case, but to help the community to engage in facing up to complex problems and to ask the right questions. Traditionally, we have looked to leaders to provide answers; asking questions implies the leader does not have the answers, which can undermine the community's confidence in the leadership. This alternative view of leadership carries with it considerable risk. Followers often look to the leader to rescue them from whatever difficulty besets them. In the case of a wicked problem, the leader's role is to make followers face their responsibility. This is unlikely to be something they readily accept or embrace, though I have seen it successfully implemented in some schools, in a limited way. In a self-improving system, which is expected to be the architect of social mobility, equality and raised aspirations, all systems must play their part.

When we think about the environment that gives children the best chance to flourish, it includes healthcare, appropriate housing, a stable home life, a culture that values education, local employment, and parents and carers who have the capacity to love, nurture and give time and attention to their offspring. It will not be achieved in a generation. Developing a

---

81   Grint, K. (2008): Wicked Problems and Clumsy Solutions: the Role of Leadership. *Clinical Leader*, 1 (2). Stockport: The British Association of Medial Managers.

society that enables mental and physical flourishing for all its members is a multi-generational, multi-disciplinary, wicked problem that requires the co-operation of many different systems. If we can acknowledge its characteristics as a wicked problem (i.e. we will not solve it, but may be able to make it better) we may be more able to acknowledge small successes, and focus our attention on working across the interconnecting systems to make things better.

First, though, we need to start a debate involving those from across the different systems and must come to some agreement concerning what 'better' means. While for many of us, it means a more equal society and greater social mobility: we still operate within a system that affords *Success to the Successful*.[82] We allocate resources to group A (those already doing well) on the understanding that they will in part use those resources to support group B (those doing less well) until group B is elevated to the status of group A. This works just as long as the resources allocated to group A exceed what they need for their own survival. In a world of finite resources, where A and B are ultimately in competition, and those in group A are privileged with assigning the resources, there will always be winners and losers.

Implications for school leaders' resilience

While the political system focuses on short-term success, leaders who are struggling are likely to continue to find it hard to trust the system sufficiently to ask for help. When faced with disease, Maté asks a question that prompts a systemic response: 'Why does **this** patient have **this** disease **now?**'[83]

If we were to ask the same question of a school that is struggling, and take into account all the inter-related systems that impact on a single student's attainment – as well as the efforts of leaders in addressing the challenges of raising attainment in a particular community – we might be more inclined to approach these wicked problems with compassion and understanding, and to learn from failure. Individual leaders might be more able to see themselves as cogs in the wheel of the education system, rather than

---

82   Goodman, M. & Dutton, J. (2012): Success to the Successful. In Senge, P. et al. *Schools that Learn* (pp. 372-375). London: Nicholas Brealey.
83   Maté, G. (2003): *When the body says no*. Toronto: Random House, p. 242.

mechanics charged with fixing the individual components of the engine, to be removed when too many components fail at the same time.

Leaders who have a realistic view of their own sphere of influence are far more likely to be able to recover from setbacks and learn from their mistakes, than those who are seduced into the self-sabotaging belief that they are ultimately responsible (as distinct from 'accountable') for an individual student's success. The education system alone cannot solve the country's educational challenges. Individual headteachers, teachers and schools do their best to promote a climate where learning can take place, risks can be taken and mistakes made in a culture of safety and acceptance. At the same time, demands from society and the voice of government promote a climate that is anything but safe and accepting. Not only do headteachers operate in this climate, many also take on responsibility for shielding their school community from its effects.

If you are a school leader who sees yourself as 'not good enough', picking up responsibility for the failings of many interconnected systems over many years will readily confirm your sense of failure. What is required to sustain and strengthen resilience in school leadership, I propose, is a change in the system to allow fear of failure to be replaced by trust in collaborative endeavour and a commitment to lifelong learning. If our goal were to build a community of lifelong learners, perhaps we would be less preoccupied with the imperative to achieve academic qualifications within a specific timescale, and less inclined to measure the success of a school by its position in league tables. When leadership in a school is judged to have failed, more often than not the professional with ultimate accountability for the school is dismissed. There is no close analysis of the factors that contributed, no question of – to use Maté's approach – why this leader, in this school, now? I constantly remind my coaching clients who are inclined to dwell on their failures, that they should also note and analyse what they have done well, in order to be able to replicate success, rather than simply to avoid failure. It seems that the education system suffers from the opposite malaise, so determined to learn from success that it neglects the importance of learning from failure.

We are very good at looking at what contributes to success. Successful schools are held up as beacons of good practice and case studies identify what it is that they do in order that we can learn from them. System leaders are those who have a 'badge' indicating they have a role in leading a school judged by Ofsted as successful. There is a collective will to disregard factors that contribute to failure and it is left to individuals who have the courage, to be open and reflective about what went wrong with their leadership in order to give others the opportunity to learn from their mistakes. It is rare for school leaders to share the story of their own struggle, as James Hilton has done.[84] We avoid staring failure in the face and tracing the lines back to the events that caused them. We collude in a collective sweeping under the carpet of the dust of failure, in case we should learn something that would force us to call into question some of the sacred cows that we have learned to worship. We ignore the lessons of 'black box thinking' prevalent in the aviation industry where 'failure is not regarded as an indictment of the specific pilot who messes up, but a precious learning opportunity for all pilots, all airlines and all regulators'.[85] Pilots are rewarded for reporting 'near misses' as long as they do so quickly; investigative reports are widely shared in order that the system can learn from them.

Systems influence and are influenced by those who operate within them. We abdicate our responsibility if we simply blame the system and do nothing to change it. We have a collective responsibility to challenge an education culture where fear of failure prevents learning. Throughout the book, I have shared examples of what professionals who are held accountable for the success of institutions might do to sustain resilience.

If you are in that position, and have arrived here via the rest of the book, you will know the importance of:

- being aware of, and prioritising what supports your own resilience.
- looking after your own wellbeing: putting the oxygen mask on yourself first.
- managing your energy and practising self-compassion.

---

84 Hilton, J. (2016): *Leading from the Edge.* London and New York: Bloomsbury Publishing.
85 Syed, M. (2015): Black Box Thinking. London: John Murray.

- acting from a position of autonomy: reviewing the habits of behaviour and thinking that you learned in childhood, which may no longer serve you.

- reflecting honestly on what you can influence first-hand or through influencing a third party; and what is beyond your reach: focusing on the former and letting go of the latter.

As we have seen, many of us are connected with the education system, either first hand or through other systems. You do not have to be working in a school to influence the system. Any of us can contribute by:

- acknowledging the pressures of school leadership.

- acknowledging the difference that we have made, even if we deem it 'not enough'.

- being a role model for encouraging wellbeing.

- having the courage to share our concerns and inadequacies where appropriate.

- exploding the myth of the superhero.

- valuing our own failure as an opportunity to learn.

Each of us has the potential to act as educators in our daily lives. Those of us who work in the education system are uniquely privileged. We are concerned with learning from the past and creating the future. As I consider the world in which my grandchildren will themselves become grandparents, I hope society will value learning and wisdom, compassion and integrity. If we could, collectively, today plant the seeds of an education system that truly acknowledges the place of failure in learning, what might its contribution be to building a more compassionate and generous society in which our grandchildren's grandchildren can flourish?

Learning from the past and creating the future

Suggestions for Further Exploration

I hope it has become apparent that building emotional resilience is not an event, but a commitment to a lifestyle that includes reflection and learning, establishing boundaries and being able to choose our responses to our experience. Below are some resources that you may find helpful if you choose to build on your learning.

Working alone

References point you in the direction of further reading and I list below resources that I have not referenced but which may be useful to you.

Casserley, T, and Megginson, D. (2009): *Learning from Burnout*. Oxford: Elsevier.

Clarkson, P. (1994): *The Achilles Syndrome*. Shaftesbury: Element.

Day, C, and Schmidt, M. (2007): Sustaining Resilience. *Developing Sustainable Leadership*, pp. 65-86. London: Sage.

Flintham, A. (2003a): *Reservoirs of Hope*. Nottingham: NCSL.

Flintham, A. (2003b): *When Reservoirs Run Dry*. Nottingham: NCSL.

Kabat-Zinn, J. (1994): *Wherever you go, there you are*. London: Piatkus

Steward, J. (2014): Sustaining emotional resilience for school leadership.

School Leadership & Management: Formerly School Organisation, 34 (1), pp. 52-68.

Walker, R. (2007): *Leading Out of Who You Are*. Carlisle: Piquant Editions.

Web resources

www.brenebrown.com/videos

www.mindtools.com

www.robertsoncooper.com/gooddayatwork

www.self-compassion.org

www.valuescentre.com

Download the Five Ways to Wellbeing app based on the New Economics Foundation's findings for free from the Google play and Apple App Store

Download the Headspace app for daily meditation practice from www. headspace.com

Working with others

One-to-one

Find a qualified coach via a reputable coaching organisation, such as the European Mentoring and Coaching Council or the International Coach Federation. Coaching takes place in a non-judgemental environment and allows you to do your best thinking. Try to contact more than one possible coach at a time, have a conversation with each so that you can decide which you feel most comfortable with.

Working in groups

Visit www.chrysalisleadershipdevelopment.com to find out about forthcoming resilience workshops, or to discuss coaching.

Undertake an eight-week Mindfulness Based Stress Reduction course with a reputable provider.

For a list of practitioners of Franz Ruppert's methods, go to www. healthy-autonomy-centre.co.uk

References

ATL, DfES, GMB, NAHT, NASUWT, NEOST & PAT. (2003): *Raising Standards and Tackling Workload*. Available at: www.dera.ioe.ac.uk/540/1/081210thenationalagreem enten.pdf

Barrett, R. (1998): *Liberating the Corporate Soul*. Woburn, MA: Butterworth Heinemann.

Barrett, R. (2010): *The New Leadership Paradigm*. US and UK: The Values Centre.

Barrett, R. (2017): *Stages of Psychological Development*. Available at: www.valuescentre. com/sites/default/files/uploads/The_Seven_Stages_of_Psychological_Development.pdf

Baumeister, R. F. (2003): Ego depletion and self-regulation failure. *Clinical and Experimental Research*, 27(2), 281-84.

BBC Television. (1 June 2017): *The Truth about Sleep*. Available at: www.bbc.co.uk/ programmes/p05lyc7s [Accessed: 18 July 2017].

Bennis, W. & Goldsmith, J. (1997): *Learning to Lead*. London, UK: Nicholas Brealey.

Berne, E. (1961): *Transactional Analysis in Psychotherapy*. New York, NY: Grove Press.

Blanchard, K. (2011): *The One Minute Manager Meets the Monkey*. London, UK: Harper Collins.

Boyatzis, R. E. (2006): An overview of intentional change from a complexity perspective. *Journal of Management Development*, 26 (7), 607-623.

Broughton, V. (2014): *Becoming Your True Self*. Steyning, UK: Green Balloon Publishing.

Cooper, C. L. & Hupert, F. A. (2014): *Wellbeing: A Complete Reference Guide, Volume 6*. Chichester, UK: John Wiley & Sons Ltd.

Covey, S. (1989): *The 7 Habits of Highly-Effective People*. London, UK: Simon & Schuster.

Cropley, M. (2015): *The Off Switch*. London, UK: Virgin Books.

Cuddy, A. (2015): *Presence*. London, UK: Orion.

Culpin, V. (2018): *The Business of Sleep*. London, UK: Bloomsbury.

Daniels, D. N. & Price, V. A. (2009): *The Essential Enneagram*. New York, NY: HarperCollins.

Department for Education (DfE). (2010): *The Importance of Teaching*. London, UK: HMSO.

Foster, R. (17 March 2017): *BBC iplayer radio*. Available at: www.bbc.co.uk/programmes/b08hz9yw [Accessed: 22 March 2017].

Frankl, V. E. (2004): *Man's Search for Meaning*. London, UK: Ebury Press, Random House.

French, S. (2009): *The NAHT Worklife Balance Survey 2008-2009*. Available at: www.naht.org.uk

Goleman, D. (1988): *Working with Emotional Intelligence*. London, UK: Bloomsbury.

Goodman, M. & Dutton, J. (2012): Success to the Successful. In Senge, P. et al. *Schools that Learn* (pp. 372-375). London, UK: Nicholas Brealey.

Government Office for Science. (2008): *Mental Capital and Wellbeing Summary*. London, UK: HMSO.

Grint, K. (2008): Wicked Problems and Clumsy Solutions: the Role of Leadership. *Clinical Leader*, 1(2). Stockport, UK: The British Association of Medial Managers.

Hammersley-Fletcher, L. (2013): Value(s)-Driven Decision Making. *Educational Management, Administration and Leadership*, 43(2).

Harris, B. (2007): *Supporting the Emotional Work of School Leaders*. London, UK: Paul Chapman.

Hay McBer. (2000): *Research into Teacher Effectiveness*. London, UK: DfEE.

Hilton, J. (2016): *Leading from the Edge*. New York, NY: Bloomsbury Publishing.

Hollis, J. (2005): *Finding Meaning in the Second Half of Life*. New York, NY: Gotham Books.

Reivich, K. J., Seligman, M. E. P. & McBride, S. (2011): Master Resilience Training in the US Army. *American Psychologist*, 66(1).

Kolappa, K., Henderson, D. C. & Kishore, S. P. (1 January 2013): No physical health without mental health. *Bulletin of the World Health Organisation*, 3-3A.

Kroese, F. M. (2016): Bedtime procrastination. *Journal of Health Psychology*, 21(5), pp. 853-862.

Lewis, P. A. (2013): *The Secret World of Sleep*. New York, NY: Palgrave Macmillan.

Marsh, H. (2014): *Do No Harm: Stories of Life, Death and Brain Surgery*. London, UK: Weidenfeld & Nicolson.

Maslow, A. (1965): Self-Actualization and Beyond. *Proceedings of the Conference on the Training of Counselors of Adults* (pp. 108-131). Available at: http://files.eric.ed.gov/fulltext/ED012056.pdf [Accessed 26 October 2017].

Maté, G. (2003): When the body says no. Toronto, Ontario: Random House.

Maxwell, A. & Riley, P. (2017): Emotional demands, emotional labour and occupational outcomes in school principals. *Educational management, administration and leadership*, pp. 484-502.

Mental Health Taskforce. (2016): *The Five Year Forward View for Mental Health*. London: NHS England. Available at: www.england.nhs.uk/wp-content/uploads/2016/02/Mental-Health-Taskforce-FYFV-final.pdf

Mischel, W. (2014): *The Marshmallow Test*. London, UK: Transworld Publishers.

Neff, K. (2011): *Self Compassion*. New York, NY: HarperCollins.

Oxford University Press. (2012): *Paperback Oxford English Dictionary 7th Edition*. Oxford, UK: Oxford University Press.

Patterson, J. L. & Kelleher, P. (2005): *Resilient School Leaders*. Alexandria, VA: Association for Supervision and Curriculum Development.

Plsek, P. E. & Greenhalgh, T. (2001): The challenge of complexity in health care. *BMJ Clinical Research*, 323(7313), pp. 625-628.

Robertson, I. T., Cooper, C. L., Sarkar, M. & Curran, T. (2015): Resilience training in the workplace from 2003 to 2014. *Journal of Occupational and Organizational Psychology*, pp. 533-562.

Ruppert, F. (Ed.) (2016): *Early Trauma* (English Language Edition ed.). (J. Stuebs, Trans.) Steyning, UK: Green Balloon Publishing.

Schüpbach, A. P. (2010): Longitudinal effects of emotional labour on emotional exhaustion and dedication of teachers. *Journal of Occupational Health Psychology*, 15(4), pp. 494-504.

Segerstrom, S. & Ness, S. L. (2007): Heart Rate Variability Reflects Self-Regulatory Strength, Effort and Fatigue. *Psychological Science*, 18(3), pp. 275-281.

Seligman, M. (2006): *Learned Optimism* (Vintage ed.). New York, NY: Vintage Books.

Senge, P. (1992): *The Fifth Discipline*. Toronto, Ontario: Random House.

Senge, P. (2004): *The leader's new work: Building Learning organisations*. In K, Starkey, S, Tempest and A, McKinlay (eds). How organisations learn: Managing the search for knowledge (pp. 462-486). London, UK: Thomson.

Shah, S. A. (2012): *Well-being patterns uncovered*. London, UK: New Economics

Foundation.

Smith, C. & Davidson, H. (2014): *The Paradox of Generosity.* New York, NY: Oxford Universtiy Press.

Syed, M. (2015): *Black Box Thinking.* London, UK: John Murray.

The Young Foundation. (2009): *Sinking and Swimming: Britain's Unmet Needs.* London, UK: The Young Foundation.

van der Kolk, B. (2014): *The Body Keeps the Score.* London, UK: Allen Lane.

Ware, B. (2011): *The Top Five Regrets of the Dying.* London, UK: Hay House.

West-Burnham, J. (2009): *Rethinking Educational Leadership.* London, UK: Continuum International Publishing Group.

World Science Festival. (17 February 2015): *How we bounce back: The new science of human resilience.* Available at: www.youtube.com/watch?v=XXRsQFDgnX8&t=6s [Accessed 18 February 2017].

Yalom, I. D. (2008): *Staring at the Sun.* San Francisco, CA: Jossey-Bass.

Index

(